Why V

by

John Weyland

authorHOUSE®

AuthorHouse™
1663 Liberty Drive
Bloomington, IN 47403
www.authorhouse.com
Phone: 1-800-839-8640

Published by AuthorHouse 3/2/2012

ISBN: 978-1-4685-3173-2 (e)
ISBN: 978-1-4685-3174-9 (sc)

Library of Congress Control Number: 2011962958

Contents

I.

Why The World Is Moving Toward Becoming An All-inclusive Welfare State

Chapter 1

The world is moving toward becoming an all-inclusive welfare state.

Chapter 2

The unique history of the human species explains why the world is moving toward becoming an all-inclusive welfare state.

The crucial element in that history is the development of imagination. It is imagination that makes human beings care what happens to other human beings outside their own families.

Chapter 3

Imagination evolved to enable human beings to think.

Thinking without imagination is impossible. Because thinking requires considering—which is imagining—alternatives.

This is a more effective way of dealing with situations than instinct. Because it is more adaptable. That is why it evolved.

Chapter 4

While imagination evolved to enable human beings to think, it had side effects. Which turned out to have very important consequences in human history.

John Weyland

Chapter 5

Imagination caused human beings to share the feelings of others.

They did not have the feelings themselves. What caused the feelings in others was not causing the feelings in them. That was done by imagination. With imagination they put themselves in the place of others and felt what they imagined those others were feeling.

The capacity to share the feelings of others like this is unique with the human species.

Chapter 6

Imagination enabled human beings to identify with others that they were not naturally identified with.

Many other creatures naturally identify with others. They have a biological relationship with them. Because of that biological relationship they treat those others differently than they do the rest of their species.

Human beings have been naturally identified with others. They had a biological relationship with them. But with imagination they were able to identify with others with whom they did not have this biological relationship. They could imagine relationships which substituted for the biological relationships.

Chapter 7

The unique capacities human beings had to share the feelings of others and identify with others helped cause the human family.

Presumably, human females originally had special relationships only with their young. And fed them and

4

cared for them only until they were big enough to look after themselves. That would have been typical with mammals. It was instinctual.

At some time during the primitive age human females and males began living together. This, presumably, because of the males' capacity for year-round sex. They wanted to be with females.

The males began to share responsibility for feeding and otherwise caring for the young. This made possible the longer childhood for human young. And the family that consisted of a male and female and young of different ages.

This was not instinctual. It depended upon feelings developing within families. Especially among males. Feelings that could have developed only because of human imagination.

Chapter 8

For most of their existence human beings did not take any responsibility for human beings outside their own families.

They lived in small groups that consisted of their own families. These separate families within any given area were enemies because they were all trying to survive within those areas. Which did not provide them with enough to keep them all alive.

Human beings can change their feelings toward one another to fit the circumstances. If they are enemies, they can suppress their capacity to share one another's feelings. If they are enemies, they do not identify with one another. The situation is the opposite of when they take responsibility for one another. As they do within their own families.

These hostile small groups existed throughout most of the primitive age. Which was by far the longest age for the human species.

Chapter 9

Toward the end of the primitive age human beings developed language, which changed their relations with some of those outside their own families.

The development of language can be dated approximately. It happened less than 100,000 years ago.

The development of language can be dated approximately because it caused tribes. Tribes left evidence of their existence.

Human beings undoubtedly communicated by sounds with one another much earlier. But language is different from this. Language makes possible large-scale, complicated communication. Which only human beings are capable of.

Language caused tribes because with it human beings could identify with some of those outside their own families. They no longer belonged to just their own families. They belonged to tribes as well.

Tribes made possible larger groups of human beings. But not much larger. Because any given area could provide food for only a limited number.

With tribes human beings could not only identify with one another. They could share the feelings of others outside their own families. And act on those feelings. The world around them no longer consisted of only enemies.

Tribes were a breakthrough for the human species. They represented a new kind of relationship. But they had nothing like the revolutionary effect of agriculture. Human being still lived from hand to mouth. They still lived in relatively small groups. The limitation of identity to immediate families was ended, but otherwise life went on very much as it had before.

Chapter 10

Agriculture ended collective responsibility.

The human species had practiced collective responsibility since the origin of the family. Family members shared with one another. They looked after one another.

Agriculture ended collective responsibility because it introduced minority rule. (Besides minority rule agriculture introduced larger groups (states), hierarchy, inequality, exploitation, inheritance, and war—all characteristics of human life since.)

The ruling minorities wanted as much as possible for themselves. And were in a position to get it. This ruled out collective responsibility. The ruling minorities were concerned with others only insofar as they benefited the ruling minorities. If they did not, they had to look after themselves.

Except that—

Charity was practiced in all the agriculture states. The members of these states had a sense of identity with one another. It was an artificial sense of identity, not a biological sense of identity. (Though it was often represented as that.) That sense of identity enabled the members of these states to share the feelings of others. Because of that they would sometimes help those others. But whether they did or not was voluntary. And even if involuntary, as sometimes happened, it was limited. Help did not have to be given to all who needed it. Charity was not large-scale enough to be collective responsibility.

Chapter 11

The Industrial Revolution ended the minority rule of the agricultural age.

That is why it eventually produced the welfare state.

The minority rule of the agricultural age was absolute. Minorities were able to use force to take whatever they wanted for themselves.

It was this situation that determined the morality of the agricultural age. As it was practiced. Not as it was preached. The morality that was preached was the morality of brotherhood. Brotherhood being another way of expressing collective responsibility. But the practice of this morality had to be postponed to an afterlife, since it could not be practiced to any significant extent in this life.

Minority rule was not replaced by majority rule in the modern age. Minorities were still able to get more for themselves than others. Get more economically, politically, and socially. But their rule was no longer absolute. They had to share it with majorities. It was no longer based entirely on force. There was an element of choice.

The compromise was that majorities got less than minorities. But under the welfare state they were guaranteed enough, even at the lowest level, to get by. With a standard of living somewhat above mere subsistence. (Just how much varied from country to country.)

This compromise satisfied the feeling for collective responsibility inherited from the primitive age.

There had been a movement for real equality, but this had been discredited by systems which put it into effect. These systems did not work efficiently or satisfactorily, because they turned out to be reversions to minority rule. Once again, it was force which determined how what was available was divided up. And everything else.

Chapter 12

Support for the welfare state is selfish.

Not only by those who gain from it. But by those who lose from it.

Philanthropy has traditionally been seen as the opposite of selfishness. Which it is in one sense. But which it is not in another sense.

Because of imagination human beings feel pain when others feel pain. And they feel pleasure when others feel pleasure. The pain and pleasure they feel through imagination is not the same as the pain and pleasure they feel themselves. But they do really exist. And they do enter into choices about behavior.

So when human beings practice philanthropy, as they do in supporting the welfare state, they are being selfish. This form of selfishness may be praised as different than the other form, but it is still selfishness.

Chapter 13

The welfare state deprived charity of its excuse for not helping all those who needed help.

Anyone giving charity could rightly say that he could not help all those who needed help. No matter how rich he might be. And organizations could use the same excuse. Though they could help more, they could not help all.

This excuse enabled individuals and organizations to deal with the logical objection to charity. Which was why give charity to some and deny it to others? If some deserved it, why not all? The answer was that giving charity to all who deserved it was impossible. So some had to be denied. There was no choice.

The difference with the welfare state was that it could provide charity to all those who needed it. This was proven by the many countries that became welfare states. The excuse for excluding some was no longer valid. Charity for all had become practical.

Chapter 14

Political realities promoted the feeling of common humanity—and so the practicality of an all-inclusive welfare state.

With the coming of the Industrial Revolution peoples moved about move. Particularly to parts of the world that had been unknown to Europe.

The outstanding example of this took place in what came to be known as the United States of America.

The nations of Europe were largely made up of peoples who thought of themselves as separate and distinct. The United States was different. Its population was made up of peoples from different nations in Europe, plus Africans brought over as slaves. This population gave itself an artificial identity. That was easier because while the immigrants came from various nations, they shared what was essentially a common culture. Which the Africans were obliged to accept.

After World War II the immigration changed. Peoples came from different cultures. And they differed physically. The Africans created a partly separate identity for themselves. This forced the United States, since it was a democracy, to accept diversity. The definition of an American became anyone living in America, and all cultures, as well as all physical types, were proclaimed to be equal.

Since the United States was the greatest power in the world and its culture the most popular, this new view of humanity spread. Human beings were given more and more to identify themselves with all other human beings. It helped greatly that they knew more about each other than they ever had before, and so could identify more easily.

This new state of affairs made indifference toward the welfare of foreign populations more difficult to maintain.

There was a tendency to feel more responsible for them. And so to believe they should be helped if they needed help.

Chapter 15

Evidence that the world is moving toward an all-inclusive welfare state is that countries now extend charity to other countries in the way they used to extend charity only to their own populations.

Not until the 20th century did countries begin extending charity to one another. Prior to that countries did not concern themselves with the internal problems of populations in other countries. They assumed each country was responsible for the welfare of its own population.

The first acts of international charity were in response to disasters. Not to chronic problems in other countries. Later, charity came to include trying to improve conditions to enable populations in other countries to better themselves. But not to give welfare to them outright.

International charity would not have taken place, obviously, without a change in attitude in the countries involved.

The feeling of common humanity had been limited to religion. Human beings felt obliged to share their religions, which they believed offered salvation. And they considered salvation to be more important than anything else. But their concern did not extend to the material welfare of others. They might have wished it was greater, but it never occurred to them to intervene. (Unless the intervention was linked to religion.)

Religion declined. Human beings came to feel more concern about welfare than religion. And to get to know much more about the lives of those outside their own countries. That knowledge—particularly knowledge gained through what they saw on television—inclined them more to put themselves in the place of those others. A larger feeling of common humanity developed.

And war stopped being inevitable for the first time since the start of the agricultural age. Typically, war had been the only way to get more. There was only so much to go around. For one country to increase its share, some other country had to lose some of its share. The Industrial Revolution changed this. Because production could be increased, it became possible for one country to get more without another country getting less.

War had blocked the feelings that caused the sense of common humanity. The populations of other countries had to be hated. Without war that hatred no longer had to be there. Human beings could have a different attitude toward other human beings.

Chapter 16

The cost of an all-inclusive welfare state can seem too great. But with time it probably will not be.

With present conditions there are too many poor. But their numbers are likely to decline. The prevailing belief is that the opposite will happen. That the poor will go on being poor. And will continue to have many children, which will help keep them poor.

The global economy looks for cheap labor. But it pays cheap labor better than that labor can otherwise get. Otherwise the jobs would not be taken.

When cheap labor gets paid better, it lives better. It can. The standard of living is very low compared to advanced countries, but it still leaves enough to provide more than bare subsistence. Families can buy things they could not buy before. This gives them the choice between more things and more children. A large majority choose more things.

And the fewer children become better educated. Their

parents have more money to spend on them. They do not have to be put out to work. When these fewer children grow up, they get better jobs. They earn more than their parents. They have more to spend on educating their children. Who then go on to earn more than they do. Each generation is better-off than the previous one.

So the cost of all-inclusive welfare should go down. As the number of the poor goes down.

Chapter 17

Countries are willing to spend more on welfare than on charity.

This is partly because they do not have the excuse with charity that not everybody can be helped. But it is also because, unlike with charity, they do not know how much welfare is costing them personally. And they do not have control over that amount.

Everybody knows how much he gives in charity. At some point the individual will say that is enough and more would be too much. The individual makes the decision. Nobody knows how much he gives in welfare. And the individual does not control that amount. The individual can try to exercise some control through the political system, but the extent of his actual control is minuscule.

Which means that the public is more generous with welfare than with charity. Not only do they now know how much they are giving, but they tend to think that others are bearing more of the cost than they are. Because that is what they want to think, and they do not have the information that would prove them wrong.

Chapter 18

The cost of an all-inclusive welfare state will come down. The willingness to bear the cost will be greater than it would be if the public were fully informed. And the generosity of the public is greater than it might seem.

Human beings are selfish when it comes to getting money. This is not only because they want more. It is because they have to be selfish when they are competing with others. Which they are most of the time. With competition human beings produce as much as they can to get as much as they can. The behavior that competition forces on human beings is often taken to be evidence that they are selfish by nature. Which they are. But at the same time they are unselfish. The human family would not exist if human beings were only selfish. They are selfish in getting money in large part so they can be unselfish in what they do with that money.

This unselfishness is what caused charity originally and the welfare state recently. It is a powerful motivation. Powerful enough to make human beings willingly give more to others than their history would indicate they would be. Since during most of that history minority rule prevented any generosity beyond limited charity. So the all-inclusive welfare state is a real possibility. Even if the cost is greater than they now might seem willing to pay.

II.

Why Bankruptcy Has Gone From Being Very Severely Punished To Being Very Lightly Punished

Chapter I

Bankruptcy has gone from being very severely punished to being very lightly punished.

Originally, bankruptcy was punished by enslavement. Not only those who went bankrupt suffered, but all their descendants. If there were any.

This happened typically to small farmers. Since almost off of a country's population were farmers at the time, this happened very often.

Small farmers led a precarious existence. They could get by in good years, but in bad years they would find themselves without enough to live on. What they did them was to borrow from big farmers. They had no choice.

The agreements in these transactions provided that the small farmers would become slaves if they did not repay what they had borrowed. Given their precarious existences, sooner or later they were unable to repay their debts and they were enslaved. Once they were enslaved, there was no way for them to gain their freedom, since they could no longer earn money for themselves. They remained slaves. And their children, and their children's children, all their descendants, remained slaves. If there were descendants.

The big landowners did not have to depend on small farmers for slaves. They could buy soldiers from defeated armies. And women and children from defeated areas. It was an accepted practice to enslave the defeated.

Wars were fought on a large scale in the Ancient World. There was enough centralization of authority to maintain armies of thousands. This meant ever-recurring large supplies of slaves.

When slaves cost less to buy than breed, they were bought. Breeding is expensive. It takes too long for children to become workers. Slaveowners then worked their slaves harder and treated them worse, so they died off sooner. Slaves descendants became a rarity.

This situation changed with the collapse of the Ancient World. Wars could no longer be fought on a large scale. The only slaves available were local slaves. They had to be treated better so they could reproduce their numbers.

This led to serfdom. Under serfdom slavery was combined with sharecropping. The slaves had to work for the large landowners as slaves. But they were allowed to provide for themselves as small farmers who got to keep a share of what they grew and otherwise produced.

The Industrial Revolution replaced serfdom and slavery by paid work. Those who got paid to work could borrow money. They could pay it back. They had the means. But what was to be done with them if they were unable to repay what they had borrowed? They were put in prison. This could seem to be a poor solution to the problem. If they were in prison, they could not earn money and so could not pay off their debts. What did happen often was that their relatives and friends paid off their debts for them and got them out. But it also happened often that nobody could or would pay off their debts for them. They were a useless expense.

As the Industrial Revolution continued, the attitude toward bankruptcy changed. An awareness developed that borrowed money could be invested in production and so increase production. There would be more of everything. Encouraging borrowing seemed a better idea than discouraging borrowing.

One way of encouraging borrowing was to punish bankruptcy less severely. Imprisonment for not repaying borrowing was done away with. All that could happen to bankrupts was that it became harder for them to borrow money. Bankruptcy went from being severely punished to being lightly punished. It went from being a serious crime to being no crime at all.

Chapter 2

All banks could go bankrupt at any time.

That is because they always owe more than they could pay.

This characteristic of banks was developed without public knowledge. It is still not known to much of the public.

Banks owe more than they could pay because their loans exceed their deposits.

This is not a necessary situation. Bank loans could be limited to deposits. They probably were originally. But by the time the practice of loaning more than deposits was discovered by governments it had gone too far to be reversed.

Why banks loan out more than they have on deposit is very simple. They make more that way. Just how much varies with the ratio between loans and deposits. Ten to one is considered a conservative loans to deposit ratio. With ten to one banks are making ten times what they otherwise would.

This practice is inherently dangerous. Banks used to go bankrupt in large numbers. Whenever too many depositors demanded their money back.

One of these times was during the early period of the Great Depression. Governments intervened. They agreed in the future to back bank deposits when the banks could not. The idea was that if depositors knew they could get their money back they would not ask to get it back.

At the same time governments started using paper money. Real paper money. Not paper money that could be exchanged for gold. Once they did this, they could create any amount of money. So there was no danger that they could not pay off however much the banks owed to the depositors.

This seemed to guarantee that banks could not fail. But

they still could. They could earn so little they would not be able to pay what they owed to others besides their depositors. Along with not being able to pay their depositors.

When this happened governments had to give them money. Instead of just giving money to their depositors.

Governments could not let very many banks fail because bank loans were needed to keep the system working. Businesses could not keep going by just using the money they took in. Without bank loans they would spend much less and economies would produce much less. Governments did not want this. And, thanks to paper money, they had the means to prevent it.

Chapter 3

Governments no longer have to go bankrupt. They can cheat their way out of it.

Governments no longer have to go bankrupt because money has become paper money with nothing behind it. They can make any amount of this money they want and pay off all of their debts.

Paper money with nothing behind it was imposed during the Great Depression. Before that governments had used paper money, but paper money with something behind it. Gold. The paper money was supposed to be exchangeable for gold. That meant governments could print only so much paper money because they had only so much gold. They could run out of money. They could go bankrupt.

Paper money with nothing behind it was supposed to be a temporary expedient. It had been used like that before. During the American and French revolutions. During wars. Etc. When governments did not have enough real money to pay for what they bought. But the old money was brought back after these exceptional periods. Typically, because governments had turned out so much of the money with nothing behind it that it had become worthless

Governments learned their lesson from history. So during the Great Depression they did not spend so much that the paper money with nothing behind it became worthless. They did not have to. Governments could spend more than they took in, but not so much more as to make their money worthless.

With World War II the losing governments did spend too much and had to put out new paper money afterward. But the winning governments were able to limit their spending, and the spending of their populations, so that their money was still worth something. They did not have to replace it.

This paper money was permanent. Paper money with nothing behind it.

Governments could have stopped borrowing money as soon as they started printing paper money with nothing behind it. They could have printed however much they needed to pay for however mulch they spent. That would have been the end of government debts.

But governments did not do this. They went on borrowing money. More and more money.

They did this out of habit. Governments had always borrowed money.

This had an effect that was not acknowledged but one that enabled the new system to keep working. It limited inflation.

Printing money increases the supply of money. It gets bigger and bigger. Prices rise because there is more money than before to buy with. Inflation results. More money, not that much more to buy.

Borrowing money does not increase the supply of money. It increases the supply of credit. Credit, like money, can buy whatever there is to buy. But its effect is not permanent, like the effect of money. Once money is printed, it stays in circulation. It does not go away. It continues to have its effect. Credit is different. Credit is given for only a limited period. It comes into existence. It goes out of existence. It has its effect for a while. Then it no longer has that effect. Because it no longer exists. So while credit can have an inflationary effect, that effect will not last like the effect of money. It will go away.

Which means that governments can borrow without suffering the same consequences they do when they print money. They do not make this money worth less and less. Until it is worthless.

But—

Governments can borrow so much that they decide not to repay their debt. Unlike individuals and corporations, including banks, they have an option. They can cheat their way out of bankruptcy. They can lessen how much they owe—down to nothing, if they choose. They can do this by printing more money and causing inflation. Enough to that they are then willing to pay back however much they owe. To so much that they no longer owe anything.

This should have been foreseen when paper money with nothing behind it was imposed during the Great Depression. Measures should have been taken to limit governments' power to make their money worth less. But governments, understandably, did not introduce such measures. And the general public did not understand the new situation well enough to protest. Nothing happened. Governments can still lessen how much they owe to whatever degree they choose. They can still go bankrupt without legally going bankrupt.

III.

Why Memory Did Not Develop Enough To Keep Up With Human Speech

Chapter 1

The human memory did not develop enough to keep up with human speech.

This has proved a great handicap.

Human beings can remember only a small part of the speech they hear. And the little they do remember they remember imperfectly.

The human memory is suited to pre-speech. It served adequately during most of the evolution of the human species. But when human beings developed speech—real speech, not just a few sounds—their memory did not evolve according to the new demands on it.

That was because human beings developed speech so recently. Less than 100,000 years ago. Which did not allow memory time enough to evolve. Evolution being a slow process.

So human beings found themselves with a great capacity to express themselves, but with a small capacity to remember what was expressed.

Speech, nonetheless, brought tremendous progress. With speech human beings could share their knowledge. One human being could benefit from the experience of many human beings. This gave them an advantage no other species had at the time, or has ever come to have.

But the progress they made was nothing like the progress they could have made with adequate memory.

Chapter 2

Writing provided a means of remembering what memory could not remember.

This would have made up for memory's inadequacy if writing had been in general use like speech. It was not. Instead its use was very, very limited.

At the time only a small part of any population—specialists—could write. And putting speech into writing was expensive. It was not only the cost of the professional writers. It was that plus the cost of the materials needed for writing. Writing had to be done with something. It had to be on something. And it had to be kept somewhere.

So most human beings could not directly take advantage of writing. They could take advantage indirectly. Many of the advantages of writing filtered down to them. But it was not the same as if they themselves could write.

Chapter 3

Writing did not only provide a means of remembering what memory could not remember. It provided a means of thinking thoughts that human beings had not been able to think without it.

Writing could make available whatever thoughts human beings had thought of and written down. Then the human beings could have thoughts that came to them from considering the thoughts they had written down. And write down these new thoughts and then have more new thoughts from considering them. And so on. For however many new thoughts they were capable of.

Without writing this was not possible. Human beings could remember some of their thoughts and have new thoughts which came from considering them. But they could do this with only some of their thoughts, since their memories did not permit them to remember all of them. They could have fewer new thoughts.

Chapter 4

Printing made writing generally available. But slowly.

Printing made writing cheaper. And cheaper and cheaper as time went on. But still not cheap enough for the public to have access to it. General access.

And reading remained expensive. It had to be learned. Learning was a slow process. It was possible for individuals to learn reading on their own. But few did this. Most reading was learned in schools. And schools for the public did not become common until the 19th century. They became general only in the 20th century. And then only in advanced countries. Much of the world still cannot read. And so the advantages of writing are denied them. They are as dependent on memory—on inadequate memory—as their remote ancestors.

Chapter 5

As soon as human beings started talking, they found that thinking could not keep up with speech.

Thinking requires extra time in which to take place. It is impossible to listen and think simultaneously. Follow, yes. Think, no.

Thinking can be done after talking has stopped. But then there is the problem with memory. So it is impossible to think while listening and impossible to think adequately after listening. (Unless the matter being thought about is very simple.)

Chapter 6

Human beings started to live together democratically before speech was fully developed.

Human beings could communicate well enough with non-language sounds and sign language to make some group decisions. They could indicate what action they were approving or rejecting. They could indicate support or opposition. The choices were limited and simple. They did not require something as complicated as fully developed language.

The long period during which this kind of decision-making prevailed explains crowd behavior. Human beings learned to make decisions together with very little communication. They have an inherited capacity for this. A hint—a single short cry, a raised arm, facial expressions, whatever—can be enough to get all of them to take the same action.

Chapter 7

Human beings developed speech so they could live together more successfully.

Speech served survival.

The small groups human beings lived in during the primitive age were not always democratic. The dominant male once ruled. But human beings, as they became more intelligent, realized that no member of their group had strength enough to dominate them all if they combined against him. That was the end of the dominant male and the beginning of democracy.

Once democracy was established, the members of the group had to make decisions together. Speech enabled them to do that more successfully.

To make decisions together, they used speech so they could consider what was possible and decide what would be best for them.

Chaper 8

During the primitive age the limitations imposed on speech by memory and thinking were not a great handicap.

Speech could be simple and brief. The matters being dealt with were not that complicated. Because life in the primitive age was not that complicated. And, when group matters were involved, the objective was known. That was the common good. The groups members were dependent on one another. They had to be concerned about one another, not just themselves or some sub-part of the group.

So longer speeches and much thinking were not needed. Memory was adequate. Thinking could cope without writing.

Chapter 9

The situation of the human species changed drastically with the agricultural age.

The agricultural age introduced larger groups, minority rule, hierarchy, exploitation, inequality, inheritance and war.

Members of the group could no longer come together daily. They lived too far apart. They no longer made decisions about what the group should do. There was a ruler who made those decisions and imposed them on the group. There was no longer a common good. The good that mattered was the good of the ruling minority. The practices of daily life were meant to serve that good.

A single ruler was accepted by the ruling minority because they had to act together. That was where their strength came from.

If that is not taken into account, the system can seem to be very imperfect. The single ruler could be incompetent. He occupied the position because of inheritance. There was nothing to guarantee that inheritance would produce a good ruler. The single ruler could mistreat members of the ruling minority, which he was dependent on. It could overthrow him at any time. But despite these imperfections, the system lasted thousands of years and rulers were seldom overthrown. The explanation was the need for unity. Unity to exploit the other members of the group. Unity to defend the group against other groups. Since inequality was introduced, there was always something to fight over. Each group had to defend what it had. And try to get more. Because as time went on groups got bigger and bigger and stronger and stronger. They had to to survive.

In this system there was no place for speech like the democratic speech of the primitive age. So the problems with speech, once again, did not matter very much. (Except for brief periods in Greece and Rome, when there were forms of popular government.)

Chapter 10

The problems of speech came to matter very much in modern democracies.

Speeches are given in modern democracies to influence public opinion. Speeches do not rely on thinking to make their argument. Given the problems of speech, thinking is not suitable. Audiences would not remember enough to follow thinking. And they would not have time for it while the speech was taking place. So speakers have to have an alternative to thinking. Their alternative is feeling.

Audiences can follow feeling during a speech. It does not require memory. And feeling can and does take place while a speech is being given. It does not have to be put off until afterward.

The argument in speeches is presented as if it were based on thinking. An argument cannot be persuasive if it is presented as contrary to thinking. That would be equivalent to saying the argument is false, and no audiences will accept an argument that is acknowledged to be false.

This poses a problem. The solution for the speaker is to present the argument as if it were based on thinking, but not to go into the thinking itself. Since the actual thinking is not known, it cannot be questioned. Accepting it or rejecting it then depends on the feeling which the speech arouse.

The result is that in modern democracies public opinion is irrational, in so far as it is determined by speeches. And the determination by speeches is more considerable than might have been anticipated. Given the literacy rates in modern democracies, speeches are unnecessary. All presentations meant to influence public opinion could be made in writing. The problems of speech could be avoided. But speeches continue to be relied on. In part because speakers know they can succeed with irrational arguments when they have no rational arguments. And in part because human beings prefer speech to writing, since they have used it so much longer and find it comes more naturally to them.

Chapter 11

Public speech in modern democracies is not free.

Private speech in modern democracies is free.

Freedom of public speech is proclaimed in modern democracies. But it does not exist. This is not fully realized by the public because the means of controlling public speech in modern democracies are not the same as the means used by authoritarian governments.

Authoritarian governments control speech by treating speech they do not want as a criminal act and punishing it accordingly. Democratic governments do not control speech like that. They do not take legal action against public speech. Legally, speech is free.

The control of public speech in modern democracies is exercised by pressure groups. They block access to public speech by those who are for what they are against. When they can. And they often can.

Only a very small part of a country's population can have access to public speech. That is because the means of public speech are very limited. Those who control those means control what gets through to large numbers.

Pressure groups can determine that with votes and money. They would not exist if they did not have the capacity to do that.

When speakers violate the code imposed by pressure groups, they are condemned and not given further access to the means of public speech. This effectively silences them. They can continue to say whatever it was that got them condemned, but they can do that only in private speech.

Private speech is free in modern democracies because it does not reach large numbers and so does not have the potential to determine public opinion. That it is free leads much of the public to believe speech in general is free. In contrast to countries with authoritarian governments, where both private and public speech are not free.

Public speech was never free. Authoritarian governments enforce conformity. It was different with democratic governments. They had to allow some freedom of speech. Democracy could not function if conformity was enforced. But all democracies allowed freedom of speech only within certain limits. Those limits were set primarily by custom and religion. This is not so in modern democracies. Custom no longer had the power it once did. Custom has changed. And the strength of custom was that it did not change. Religion has declined. It used to rule lives. Now it is little more than a vestige, and the prospect is that it will get weaker and weaker. This has given the pressure groups the opportunity to set the limits on free speech that they want. The purpose of those limits is, of course, to determine behavior. By condemning what they are against and banning support for it. And praising what they are for.

Chapter 12

The new technology has greatly increase the availability of writing. But that has helped with only half the thinking problem.

Thinking can follow a written argument. But thinking cannot test a written argument unless it stops following that argument long enough to do the testing. Testing against experience and testing against logic. The two tests the argument has to pass to be valid. That takes time.

This testing is like doing a laboratory experiment. But it is done with memory and imagination, not with equipment.

Writing has generally been treated as if it were speech. As if it were to be read continuously, as listening is done continuously with speech. The reader might go back occasionally to make sure he remembered a certain passage correctly. But seldom, if ever, does he go back as often as he would have to to test every part of an argument. He forfeits the indispensable opportunity writing offers him.

The new technology will not change this. So it is unlikely to improve thinking, except for what comes from the availability of more material.

IV.

Why The Human Species Sacrificed Sex To The Single Family

Chapter 1

The human species sacrificed sex to the single family.

This happened at the beginning of the agricultural age.

Agriculture made it possible for human beings to live together in larger groups. Once this became possible, it became necessary because these groups fought one another. Numbers determined strength, and survival depended on strength.

Human beings had lived in small collectives before the agricultural age. These collectives had to be replaced because the members of the new groups were spread out over larger areas. They could not function as a single collective.

The collective survived as the family. But the families that made up the new larger groups wee not responsible for one another. Each one had to look after itself. They might sometimes help one another, but that was not the regular practice.

This system (nearly) put an end to promiscuity. Human beings are promiscuous by nature. They are sexually attracted to others of their species. They could have lived promiscuously in the agricultural age if they had established communal responsibility for children. But "they" chose the single family instead. Which reduced promiscuity to a very small level.

"They" is in quotation marks because it refers to men. Men, being stronger than women, ruled both the small collectives of the primitive age and the larger groups of the agricultural age. They made the choice for the single family.

Men chose the single family because they wanted the exclusive possession of a woman and her children. They preferred this to sharing the possession of available women and their children.

This choice imposed chastity before marriage and fidelity

after marriage on women. But at the same time it imposed sexual limitations on men. Though these limitations were not as strict for them.

Men could be promiscuous if they could find the opportunity. But that was not easy to do. The women they lived with were the daughters and wives of their neighbors. These men wanted their daughters to remain chaste, so they could get married. And they wanted their wives to remain faithful, so they could have the exclusive possession of them. For men to be promiscuous they had to violate laws which had been established to prevent just that.

This caused men to set up an institution outside of the regular system. That was prostitution. A small number of women were provided so men could have sex outside of marriage. But while this enabled men to practice some promiscuity, the degree was very limited for most. Only a very few were able to be as promiscuous as their natures dictated.

Chapter 2

Men inadvertently increased the risk of unfaithfulness.

Women had experienced estrus like other female animals. With women it was approximately every lunar month. That was the only time when they were meant to have sex.

Men were capable of having sex at any time. This was so to enable them to have sex with women whenever women wee ready to have sex. Different women were in this state at different times. They did not all experience estrus at the same time.

Because of their hands, men were capable of committing rape. They did not do this when their hands first developed. that was because they did not experience sexual desire unless the woman was in estrus. So it was the women who determined when sex took place.

But men, becoming more intelligent with time, came to realize they could enjoy sex even when women were not in estrus. That was when rape began.

In an adaptation to this new situation, women started enjoying sex when they were not in estrus.

This enabled men to have sex more often with women. Without forcing themselves on women. Year-round sex became a characteristic of the human species. But there was a drawback for men. Women could have sex with other men at any time, and could want to. So the risk of unfaithfulness was no longer limited to a few days each month. It was constant.

Chapter 3

Women support complete irresponsibility in sexual matters.

For them sex should always be available. There should be no punishment for practicing any form of it. Or for the consequences of that. Whoever incurs such consequences (pregnancy, venereal disease, etc.) should be helped by his or her fellow human beings.

Chapter 4

Traditional morality—the morality chosen by men— called for full responsibility in sexual matters.

Under traditional morality sex should not always be available. There should be punishment for practicing certain forms of it. And for the consequences of that. Whoever incurred such consequences had no claim for help from his or her fellow human beings.

The objective of traditional morality was to make the single family system work. All of the positions of traditional morality—for this, against that—were derived from this objective.

Chapter 5

Before the welfare state traditional morality prevailed.

Minority rule created traditional morality. Morality rule was the general form of government throughout the agricultural age. Minority rule was characterized by large groups, war, hierarchy, inequality, exploitation, and inheritance. Plus, of course, minority rule.

Under minority rule families had to look after themselves. Children were dependent for their livelihood on their parents and other relations. Children born outside of marriage had nobody to look after them. Except for two small exceptions. One was that those born to members of the minorities were sometimes treated as belonging to the families. The other was charity. But charity was voluntary and never met all the demands placed on it. Or even came close.

While minorities could ignore traditional morality themselves, they demanded that the majorities living under them observed it.

While the minorities would not support children outside of families, they wanted large families. Large families were in their interest. The more workers, the greater production. And they took most of production for for themselves, leaving only enough for the workers to keep them alive so they could continue working. And the more potential soldiers there were, the more wars they could fight and win. Their possessions depended on that. They took no responsibility for the soldiers when wars were not being fought.

Because the minorities wanted large families for the majorities, they opposed any limitations on births. Even though the large numbers could lead to want and starvation. The minorities profited from large numbers. They did not suffer when some of those large numbers could not stay alive. They themselves always had more than enough.

What minorities were opposed to included homosexuality and all other "unnatural" sexual activities, because those too reduced births.

The system was easy to understand. It was logical. It was enforceable. It worked.

Chapter 6

Traditional morality ended with the welfare state.

Democracy did not bring the welfare state. Originally, democracy supported traditional morality as much as minority rule had. Families were to look after their own members. Government was not to help them. Any help was to come from charity. If that was insufficient, government was still not to intervene.

The breakthrough for the welfare state came with women's suffrage. Women had been confined to families throughout the development of the human species. Their morality was family morality. Which meant sharing with others so all had enough. Which meant trying to prevent suffering in others. Women brought family morality to government. In a relatively short time after the establishment of women's suffrage, governments started helping those in need. They have been doing this on an ever-increasing scale ever since.

Chapter 7

Women first attacked the single family.

The single family had been permanent. Because outside the single family women and children had nobody to provide for them.

Women argued that some women suffered in the single family because of their dependence on their husbands. So they should be allowed to break up the family.

At the time few women were employed. The Industrial Revolution had started employment for women outside the home, but the extent of this was small. So women sought alimony and child support. Husbands were to continue providing for their (ex) wives and children after the breakup of their families.

Initially, divorce was difficult to get because of traditional morality. But it became easier as the 20th century progressed, until it was routinely granted.

Chapter 8

Women became openly promiscuous.

Women had not been promiscuous on a large scale before World War II. Their opposition to the permanent single family had not been accompanied by advocacy of promiscuity. They continued to publicly support chastity before marriage and fidelity after marriage. In practice, their public support was not matched by private support. Advances in birth control methods enabled some of them to practice promiscuity. Some of them, but far from all. The known birth control methods were used almost exclusively by better-off, better educated women. This usually prevented pregnancies, and when they happened women could resort to abortion. For them abortion, although illegal, was a recourse. It had become safer with advances in medicine. So they could practice promiscuity without providing evidence they were doing so.

The situation changed after World War II. Cheap and simple means of birth control appeared. Almost all women (in advanced countries) could practice promiscuity without becoming pregnant. They no longer saw a need for public support of traditional morality. For tem promiscuity became acceptable.

Chapter 9

Once promiscuous, women demanded support for children of unmarried mothers. And got it.

This marked the triumph of sex over the single family. Women could have sex without marriage. And not fear they would become burdened with children they could not support. Because, thanks to the welfare state, they could support as many children as they might have.

This was an easy victory for women. Once the welfare state was adopted, children born of unmarried mothers had to be supported. It was a general principle of the welfare state that all human beings it was responsible for must be supported. It was a general principle of the welfare state that all human beings it was responsible for must be supported. That had to include these children. The days when unmarried mothers were left to look after their children were over.

Not only did the welfare state have to look after these children in the sense of providing them with food and housing. It had to provide other care as well. Since their mothers worked and could not provide it themselves.

The women's movement has not dwelt on the inability of most unmarried mothers to meet the requirements of children. Particularly when they are working. It is not just the husband who has been removed from the family. It is the time the women used to have to devote to their children.

Chapter 10

Abortion represents the triumph of women.

Abortion has become anachronistic. It used to be that other means of birth control were unreliable or dangerous. Abortion could be advocated as the only practical choice. But after World War II many other means of birth control have been developed. They are not expensive. They are not complicated. Women in the modern world have to be completely irresponsible to have unwanted pregnancies. But they still insist on abortion.

The extent of women's triumph is shown by their attitude toward late-term abortion.

Human beings do not have a natural feeling against abortion before the fetus has started to look like them. There is nothing in their evolutionary history to cause them to have such a feeling. They can have an intellectual objection. Life starts at conception. The strength of women's feeling about abortion enables some of them, and some of their followers, to convince themselves that this is not so. But that is nonsense. Still, limiting abortion to the first three months of pregnancy would be a sop to popular feeling. Women could support this in the interest of reconciling abortion to the rest of the community. But women—at least the women's movements—do not do this. They press for abortion throughout pregnancy. No Limitations. There is no willingness to compromise. Which they would do if they thought their position was in any real danger. That they do not shows the extent of their triumph.

V.

Why The Decline Of Estrus Caused Homosexuality

Chapter 1

The decline of estrus caused homosexuality.

Estrus had determined when and with whom sex took place. When human females experienced estrus, human males were attracted to them. Otherwise, there was no sex.

This is how sex worked and still works in other mammals.

A difference between human females and many other mammalian females was that all human females did not experience estrus at the same time.

This had a very important consequence for human sexuality. This consequence was that human males had to be ready for sex at any time, since human females could be available for sex at any time. When human males detected estrus, they became capable of having sex.

This system stayed in force until human males evolved sufficiently to use their hands as they do now. And to use their brains more than related mammals.

Then human males began forcing sex on females when females were not experiencing estrus. Because of their hands they could do this.

The defect in the system was that human males could be stimulated to have sex by one woman experiencing estrus and force sex on another women who was not experiencing estrus.

When this happened, human males discovered they could enjoy sex when the woman was not experiencing estrus. They discovered that estrus was not a necessary part of human sexuality.

This caused the human couple. Men forced women to stay with them so they could have sex whenever they wanted. In time women learned to enjoy sex when they were not experiencing estrus. Estrus became vestigial in human females.

This development caused homosexuality became when estrus was no longer necessary for having sex, gender difference was no longer necessary for human sex. Human males and females were made so they could have sex with members of their own gender as well as members of the opposite gender.

Chapter 2

Once sex was no longer determined by estrus, homosexual sex took place. But it was bound to remain small-scale in the primitive age.

In the primitive age human beings lived together in small groups. The number of men and women was more or less equal. All adults had access to sex. Whether communal sex, or sex by couples, or some combination of the two. Despite this, some human beings would have chosen sex with their own gender, if only occasionally. Heredity is such that it can produce abnormal results, including homosexuality. But normal sex was available. It would have been preferred in most cases. The inherited behavior was there. And it had to be preferred. The survival of the small groups depended upon numbers. Exclusive homosexuality would have been fatal.

The situation changed with the agricultural age. The single family was institutionalized. This required chastity before marriage and fidelity after marriage. It was required for women, since women bore children. But the requirement for women imposed a requirement for men, since, with few exceptions, they did not have any women to be unchaste or unfaithful with.

All human beings no longer had regular access to sex. The age at which boys and girls entered puberty was too young for the agricultural age. Before they could have institutionalized sex, boys had to be capable of supporting a wife and children, and girls of looking after a family. This meant years during which both sexes had to do without heterosexual sex.

That induced homosexuality, along with other forms of abnormal sex. The extent can only be guessed at, since these forms of sex were kept secret if possible. They were forbidden. Numbers became even more important in the agricultural age than they had been in the primitive age. The agricultural age brought war and the outcome of war depended on numbers. And the agricultural age brought inequality and inequality depended on numbers. Homosexuality and other forms of abnormal sex did not produce numbers. That was why they were forbidden.

To prevent sex before marriage boys and girls were separated once they entered puberty. But while this prevented normal sex, it facilitated abnormal sex. Boys could be alone with other boys, and girls with other girls. And men with men, and women with women. The practices that went with the single family both caused the problem and offered a solution to the problem.

There is no doubt that abnormal sex was more prevalent during the agricultural age than the evidence indicates. Because it was covered up. But at the same time there is no doubt that considerable restraint was exercised. Human beings can be trained to act unnaturally. The degree of success of this training can be quite high. Sex was natural. But sex could be suppressed. That was the fate the single family imposed on human beings.

Chapter 3

War encouraged homosexuality in the agricultural age.

War had not existed in the primitive age. The small groups in which human beings lived did not have the means to fight war. They could and did fight skirmishes with neighboring groups, but these were short and infrequent.

War began in the agricultural age because agriculture provided the means to fight war. Armies had food that enabled them to operate over large distances for long periods of time.

Men were away from home. Men were living with men. Women were home. Women were living with women.

Sex does not come and go in human being as it does in other species. It is always there. It gets to be more demanding the more it is denied.

Because of war men could have sex with men or no sex. Women could have sex with women or no sex. The only alternative was sex with themselves. And war happened repeatedly. It was not something men and women could bear for a time and then be done with. It had to be adapted to as a recurring experience.

Men and women who could have preferred normal sex could have chosen homosexuality because there was not a choice. There is no doubt that this happened. The only doubt is the extent to which it happened. And the extent to which some men and women came to prefer it permanently.

Chapter 4

Women ended the condemnation of homosexuality in advanced countries.

This was part of their campaign for the all-inclusive legalization of sex.

Women had never willingly accepted the limitations men imposed on sex. Originally, they had sex whenever their nature (through estrus) told them to. When estrus became vestigial, they wanted to have sex whenever they felt like having sex. The agricultural age forced them into behavior that did not suit them. They conformed because they had to.

That they conformed led many men to think their artificial behavior was their natural behavior. Women disabused them when they got the opportunity. Starting with World War II, they began to free themselves from the limitations put on sex. Within little more than 50 years they had succeeded (in advanced countries). Not only had they gotten the prevention of pregnancy made legal, but they had done the same with abortion. And, if children were born, they were to be provided for by the state if there was no husband.

The legalization of homosexuality was included for consistency. It seemed wrong to continue to condemn homosexuality when blame was being removed from all other sexual practices.

Chapter 5

Since homosexuals are homosexuals, it would seem that homosexuality could not be inherited. But it is.

Homosexuality remains more or less constant generation after generation. As far as can be known. Admittedly, statistics were lacking until recently. But there was information that indicates the situation has not changed very much.

Homosexuality is not a condition that just pops up. There has to be a certain inclination. It has to be inborn. A man is not going to be homosexual unless he is physically attracted to other men. Or a women unless she is physically attracted to other females.

But there is ambiguity here. All men are attracted to other men. All women are attracted to other women. Most would say the attraction is not physical. Or at least not physical enough to make them want to perform the sexual acts they do with members of the opposite sex. And there is ambiguity within the ambiguity. Many otherwise normal human beings can be sexually aroused by just one member of the same sex or a few members of the same sex during a lifetime. The extent of this kind of attraction is not known. Nobody has to reveal the truth about his (or her) inner states.

The explanation for this ambiguity is that human beings do not have a satisfactory substitute for estrus. They have different reactions to the two genders, but not so different that they are always attracted only to members of the opposite sex. Without knowing it, primitive human beings sacrificed sexual certainty to more frequent sex.

Given this mixed state, human beings can generate homosexuals when they are not homosexuals themselves. It can be like the other traits which come out only when there is a certain combination of genes from the two partners. And it can be homosexuals who do not live exclusively as homosexuals. One way or the other, one new generation of homosexuals after the other gets produced. They do not die out as they would if only homosexuals could produce other homosexuals.

Chapter 6

Looking back, the wonder is that homosexuality was practiced as little as it was.

The human species imposed extreme conditions on itself. Chastity, the single family, fidelity. No other species deliberately limited its sex life. Sex is not meant to be limited. It is meant to triumph over all else. That is the whole idea. Hardship does not deter sex. Danger does not deter sex. Nothing deters sex. Even death. Evolution requires sex to be like this. The system would not work unless it was. Yet one species chose something different. And managed to abide by it. With relatively few exceptions.

Although there was an alternative. Persons of the same sex could mix together. Their activities could not be constantly supervised. Sexual relations between them would not produce evidence to condemn them. As they did with persons of different sex. Those relations caused the same body reactions as did normal relations. So homosexuality, it would seem, should have swept the human world. It could have been accepted as an institution alongside the single family. Males and females could have been homosexual before marriage and heterosexual afterwards. But this did not happen. There were instances of it, but no general acceptance. Homosexuality was never institutionalized in any civilization, even in those that came closest to tolerating it.

Homosexuality was forbidden because of the fear it would become too popular. Numbers were needed for war and production, and homosexuality did not produce those numbers.

The fear no longer exists in advanced countries. Things, not numbers, now determine the outcome of war and production. Numbers have lost their value.

There is another factor. Homosexuality used to be so dangerous because it had no other form of shared sex to compete with. Girls and women were not available. With contemporary promiscuity this is no longer so. Heterosexuality can compete with homosexuality on even terms. The results indicate that heterosexuality is proving much more popular. Homosexuality, although allowed, remains limited to a small minority.

VI.

Why Imagination
Caused A Problem With
Feelings For Others

Chapter I

Thinking caused a problem for the human species which it has not been able to solve. The problem is the feelings one human being can have for another.

Thinking caused this problem because it required imagination. It did this because in thinking choices have to be considered. To be considered they have to be imagined.

Imagination evolved in the primitive age. During much the greater part of this age imagination did not cause the problem.

Human beings lived in small groups. The feelings they had for one another were like the feelings other creatures have for other members of the groups they live in. (If that is how they live.) These feelings determined their behavior toward one another.

Human beings were not aware of the existence of more than a few other members of their species. These few were those living in their own group and in their immediate neighborhood. Toward the non-group members their normal feelings were those associated with hostility, since the small groups had to compete with one another for limited resources. Feelings of hostility prevail over other feelings in situations like this.

Imagination began to cause the feelings problems with the development of language, which came late in the primitive age. Because of language human beings could have non-hostile relations with other human beings outside their own small groups. They could communicate with them. Other creatures could not do this. The only feelings they could have were the ones nature provided them with. They could not go beyond that.

While the problem began late in the primitive age, it was small-scale then. All those sharing a language did not live together. They had to live separately to get their food. They could come together only briefly. On those occasions they could have enough food to provide subsistence for them all. Which was as much as they required and expected in the primitive age. Acts outside their groups caused by feelings could be little more than gestures.

The feelings problem did not become serious and chronic until the agricultural age.

Chapter 2

In the agricultural age human beings came to live together in larger groups. But at the same time they retained the small groups of the primitive age. These were their families.

Human beings were responsible only for the members of their families. They had natural feelings which made them want to fulfill these responsibilities. But they were also capable—because of their imagination—of feelings for other members of the larger group.

As families they did not have much to spare for the other members of that larger group, if some of those members needed help. But as a larger group they did. The agricultural age introduced surpluses. All human beings were no longer living on a subsistence level. The surpluses could have been used to help those who needed help. As imagination-induced feelings urged them to.

But this did not happen.

The larger groups of the agricultural age were ruled by minorities. These ruling minorities appropriated the surpluses for themselves. The purpose of their rule was to maximize those surpluses for themselves. There was nothing for those who needed help.

Except charity. Because of feelings for others some charity was found in all the larger groups of the agricultural age. But charity was voluntary. It came out of production only after production had been divided up. Not before.

And it was never adequate to provide help to all those who needed help. Charity did not have to be comprehensive. And it was not.

This situation lasted throughout the agricultural age. And on into the modern age. Until the development of democracy and the welfare state.

Chapter 3

All human beings experience feelings for others. But these feelings are found more in women than in men.

These feelings were essential in women. They go farther back. Women have to raise the young in mammalian species. They have to have the feelings required for that function. And these feelings carry over into imagination-induced feelings. Such feelings are stronger in women than comparable feelings in men.

This difference in the strength of feelings existed from early on in the existence of the species. From the time its members began having feelings as well as instincts.

Men eventually acquired feelings for others after they began living with women and sharing responsibility for the young. They had to to adapt to their new life. But the strength of their acquired feelings was always weaker than the strength of women's feelings.

And the differences between the two sexes became greater when they started living different lives. With the development of weapons and tools, men and women did food-getting separately. The food-getting was not just separate. It required behavior that had not been required when men and women got food together.

For hunting—which included hunting for larger animals—men had to be braver and tougher. This forced them to behave unnaturally. Bravery does not come naturally to any species. Creatures must try to avoid what is dangerous

John Weyland

for them. Otherwise they would not live very long and their species would disappear. With weapons men started doing this. Hunting big animals that were dangerous for them. But their feelings had developed earlier and were not adapted to the new behavior. That was why they had to exercise the form of self-control which is bravery.

With agriculture men hunted less or not at all. But they started fighting wars, and wars were more dangerous for them than hunting big animals. Bravery remained a requirement—even more of a requirement than before.

And other new unnatural behavior was required.

During the primitive age human beings lived in small collectives. They worked together for the common good, which was then truly the good of them all. With the agricultural age groups became larger, and the larger groups were not collectives. The collectives were the families, and they did not work together and they were not responsible for one another. Normally, they did not fight with one another, because if they did their larger groups would have become weak and would have been conquered by other larger groups. But, short of fighting (normally), they competed with one another. For what was necessary to exist. And, which was new, for more than that, because agriculture brought surplus. Not just because it produced more but because with agriculture what was produced was divided up unequally.

The competition among families was the responsibility of men. Women lived within the families. Because of that they could retain the feelings of the primitive age. But men, once again, had to adapt. They could not treat the members of other families they way they did their own family members. This meant, among other things, they could not act on their imagination-induced feelings. Not in their general behavior. They had to be hard. They could not yield to those feelings.

So men and women, with the agricultural age, came to

be different even more than they had in the primitive age. When they already had come to differ considerably.

And –

Men had to be trained to be men. Being men was not natural for them. The training occupied most of their childhood. And it did not stop when they were grown. Being men remained hard for them all their lives. So hard that many of them only partly succeeded or did not succeed at all.

Chapter 4

Imagination-induced feelings caused the brotherhood religions.

These religions—Christianity, Islam, etc.—provided the surrogate for the brotherhood that did not exist under minority rule. Because of that rule it had to be surrogate brotherhood. It could not include sharing. Except for charity, which had already existed. The scale of charity might be increased, but that was all.

Language had started the problem of imagination-induced feelings. The agricultural age greatly aggravated the problem. Human beings lived among many human beings, and knew about the existence of many more. They could feel some form of identity with a large percentage of them. Because of the same language, same area, common appearance, common traditions, common beliefs, common customs.

And, failing all else, common humanity. While feelings were aroused more readily among human beings with something in common, like language, they proved capable of feeling like brothers when the only common element was their humanity. It usually took special circumstances to bring this about. And more often than not it was overwhelmed by the opposite feelings of hostility. But common humanity could be enough by itself to provoke identification.

Chapter 5

Because minority rule made true brotherhood impossible, the new religions transferred the brotherhood they offered to another world.

Human beings believed in the existence of what did not exist. This made them susceptible to all kinds of false beliefs, like that of another world.

They believed in the existence of what did not exist because of their self. This, like imagination, developed because of thinking. Thinking required making choices. For choices to be made there had to be a choice-maker. That was the self.

The self seemed to the self to be independent of the body. Because the self used imagination to consider choices, it could do what the body could not do. It could transport itself somewhere else than where the body was. It could engage in acts that the body was not engaging in. If the body was one self, the self was a second self.

The second self did not exist like the first self did. It could not be seen, or heard, or smelled. It could not be perceived like anything else that existed could be perceived. This meant, human beings believed, there could be another form of existence. Like that of their self. It could exist while not existing. They believed their selves could inhabit that other kind of world. And could inhabit it forever. Since being separate from the body, they did not have to die.

Only recently was the truth discovered. The self does not lead an existence separate from the body. All of its activities are activities of part of the body—the brain. They are physical.

And there is an explanation for the remaining mystery of the self. How can it see and otherwise perceive what does not exist? It can because the body can see and otherwise perceive. The self sees and otherwise perceives because the body does. The seeing, etc., the self does is remembered seeing. And that seeing, etc., can be different from actual remembered seeing because the self can imagine. It can combine elements of past seeing differently than they were combined when they were actually seen.

So the human belief in the existence of what does not exist is a false belief. And that includes the belief in another world. Which is essential to the brotherhood religoins.

Chapter 6

The 20th century became the century of imagination-induced feelings in the advanced world. The 21st century will go even farther.

Advances in communications contributed to this. Like language, they enable human beings to be aware of more members of their own species. And so have more imagination-induced feelings for them.

This is particularly so because many of these advances have to do with seeing. What human beings see is more important to them than what they perceive with their other senses. They have the illusion that what they see is actually taking place in their presence. It is real to them. Whereas what they heard about, as with language, has to be imagined. What they imagine is less real to them, and so less likely to provoke responses.

Seeing want and pain elsewhere in the world has made human beings much more sensible to the suffering of common humanity. And much more inclined to do something about it.

Chapter 7

The end of minority rule made a changed morality possible.

Minority rule had prevailed throughout the agricultural age. It had determined morality. Morality was whatever behavior was most advantageous for the ruling minority.

Human beings had gotten used to this morality and considered it normal. They remembered nothing else. They were totally ignorant of the morality their forbears had lived by in the primitive age.

Starting toward the end of the 18th century, minority rule was gradually replaced by representative government. (In advanced countries.) With representative government morality came to be determined by popularity.

But there was a long period before the new situation actually caused any change. During that period morality remained what it had been.

That long period ended only after women got the vote. And only after the Great Depression. And only after World War II.

The combination of representative government and women's suffrage was not enough to make a change in morality happen. It took the Great Depression as well. Because the Great Depression started governments intrusion into the lives of their populations. That was necessary for the change in morality. It had to be implemented and enforced by government.

The Great Depression caused government intrusion because of the high and seemingly endless unemployment. In previous periods of high employment the unemployed were looked after by their families and charity. Most of the older generation still lived on farms. They could grow things and survive during depressions. And they could take in their children if need be. And if those children had gone to distant towns and cities they could return home. By the 1930s fewer of the old generation still lived on farms. And farms were more dependent on cash crops and so less-self-supporting. Going home was no longer a recourse for many of the unemployed. And charity was limited. Charity did not expand in depressions. It contracted. Because there were fewer capable of giving and most of t hem had less to give.

Because of this situation governments started providing for the unemployed. Who under minority rule would have been left to look after themselves. This initial intrusion got populations with representative governments used to accepting government intrusion. If one form was acceptable other forms seemed to be.

World War II brought more government intrusion. And so added to the acceptance of government intrusion as a part of life. But World War II saw no change in morality. That remained conventional.

The change in morality came after World War II. Women were liberated by that war because so many of them had become independent.

The change was the substitution of popularity as the determinant of morality instead of tradition. And the determinant of popularity became feeling. Feeling had always been there. It had shown itself in charity and brotherhood religions. But otherwise it had had to be repressed under minority rule.

The morality of minority rule had been rational. What it dictated could be arrived at by reason. All that had to be done was to ask what was the most advantageous morality for the minority.

The morality of popularity is irrational. Since it is determined by feeling. What feeling dictates cannot be arrived at by reasoning. Feeling is its own judge.

Chapter 8

Advanced countries became capable of acting on imagination-induced feelings to help others.

During minority rule it was impossible to act on imagination-induced feelings on a large scale. The means were not available.

Nature makes it impossible to act on imagination-induced feelings to help others. All creatures lead subsistence lives. They have nothing left over after they help those—if any—that nature tells them to help. Besides which, since they have no imagination, they have no imagination-induced feelings.

With the surpluses of the agricultural age human beings became capable of helping those outside their families. But the system ruled this out, except on a small scale. When the system was replaced in the modern age, human beings for the first time had both the opportunity and the means to extend such help.

The amount of help they provided was determined by their feelings. Seeing others in want pained them. Seeing others without some place to live pained them. Seeing others sick pained them.

The reaction, when production became sufficiently high, was to give enough to the poor so they did not seem to be suffering. This was what was done in all advanced countries.

Chapter 9

Feelings are not suited to the modern world.

They are the feelings that evolved in human beings when they lived in small collective groups. What is imagination-induced about them is when they are applied to larger numbers. But the conditions are not the same. The effects are not the same. What had appropriate effects in the small collective groups does not necessarily have appropriate effects in larger groups.

In the primitive age human beings did not have alternatives for the application of their feelings. They could help one another. But they had no capacity to apply such feelings to any other human beings outside their groups. They had no relations (except hostile relations) with those other human beings. And they had nothing to help them with if they did have any relations. Since they lived on a subsistence level.

This changed with the agricultural age. Production was increased to provide more than subsistence. But governments were not democratic. The surpluses were disposed of by ruling minorities. Their disposal was not determined by feelings.

The situations changed again with the Industrial Revolution and the modern age. Surpluses became larger. Governments became democratic. Surpluses could be disposed of by majorities. But their imagination-induced feelings did not equip them to do this for the common good (however defined). As their natural feelings had equipped them to do when they lived in small collectives.

Because in this new situation they had to deal with alternatives. They had to ask, to get optimum results (no matter how defined), whether to use the surpluses for this or for that. Which meant that had to ask whether what they were not using them for would cause more good (however defined) than what they were going to use them for. Which had not been so in the primitive age.

Majorities showed themselves incapable of dealing with this new situation. Their feelings determined what they did. They refused to try to be rational, since feelings resist being subjected to rationality. Unless necessity forces them to. And that was not so in modern democracies. Majorities could do what their feelings dictated. They did not have to think about whether alternatives would have achieved more of what they wanted. Which those alternatives often would have.

What held for helping others held for preventing or ameliorating pain in others. This is what human beings wanted to do, because pain in others caused pain in them. But doing this had consequences. Consequences that could be worse (in various ways) than what they were avoiding. As with helping others, majorities refused to subject their feelings to rationality. So what they gained could be less than what they lost.

Chapter 10

Even if human beings used their imagination-induced feelings rationally, they would not be able to solve the problem these feelings cause.

Because they could never possibly do all the things those feelings tell them to do. They could never help all the other human beings who need help. They could never prevent or ameliorate all the pain felt by other human beings.

Let alone all the other creatures these feelings tell them to feel for. Which is an extension.

Imagination did a great service for human beings when it enabled them to think. but id did a great disservice for them by enabling them to have feelings for all over human beings (and many other creatures besides). Because their inability to act on those feelings can only pain them.

It can be said that human beings themselves caused this problem. They did not have it when they lived in small groups, as nature intended them to. They came to have it only when they started living in larger groups. That was what created the problem. The insoluble problem.

VII.

Why Human Beings Became
Capable Of Expanding
Their Knowledge

Chapter 1

Before human beings could talk, they became capable of expanding their knowledge beyond their own experience.

What gave human beings this capacity was the evolution of a second kind of consciousness.

All living creatures are aware of what their bodies are telling them. They have to be to react. Without such awareness life would be impossible.

Creatures with sense organs (like human beings) are aware of what their sense organs tell them. They see, hear, smell and do whatever else their sense organs enable them to do. That is the first kind of consciousness.

Some time in their development—before they could talk—human beings developed a second kind of consciousness. This enabled them to see, hear, smell, etc., what they had sensed earlier. They could consciously remember experience.

Human beings combined this new capacity with another new capacity. This was to think. They could take the experience they had already had and combine the elements that made it up differently, anticipating what the results would be. This gave them knowledge beyond their own experience.

Chapter 2

Thinking caused the development of language.

Thinking could do very little without language. With thinking human beings could combine elements of experience differently than those elements had occurred and "see" what the results would be. But only a small part of their experience lent itself to this process. And their experience itself was very limited. And the time they could think for

71

was not very long. They could not really begin to think until they were partly grown and they did not live many years.

Before human beings developed real language they used some sounds to communicate with one another. Other species do this. What human beings did once they could think was increase these sounds. They made them correspond to the elements of their experience. Their actual experience and their imaginary experience.

They shared these new sounds with other human beings. And those other human beings shared their new sounds. The new sounds multiplied.

Before language human beings had had to almost start over again with each generation. They could pass something on through training but not much. With language they could pass on much more of their experience. And it was their collective experience, not just their individual experience.

Chapter 3

Language became supplement to evolution.

Evolution depends upon the transmission of knowledge. It accomplishes this through heredity.

The first theories of evolution concentrated on the inheritance of physical characteristics. Physical characteristics that had shown themselves to be more suitable in certain environments. More suitable meaning those with such characteristics survived at a higher rate than those without them.

The inheritance of behavior—which is the inheritance of knowledge—did not receive the same attention. But it is as important for evolution as the inheritance of physical characteristics. The neglect was due to a reluctance to accept that acquire behavior can be inherited. Including behavior acquired by the immediately preceding generation. But this had to be so. Otherwise no acquired behavior could be inherited.

Until language, evolution was taking place only through the inheritance of behavior and physical characteristics. Plus a little training in a relatively few species. With language there was a new way for evolution to take place. Because language transmits knowledge just as heredity transmits knowledge. Through heredity human beings know how to do things. Through language they find out how to do things.

Not only did language provide a new way for evolution to take place. It provided a way that proved more important than heredity. For human beings. Since human beings originated language they have become much more dependent on it for their development than any other factor.

Chapter 4

Language meant mental capacity could triumph over physical capacity.

But only under the right circumstances.

Chapter 5

Before language mental capacity was much inferior to physical capacity.

Human beings could think. Thanks to imagination. But they could not think very well. They did not have the means.

Physical capacity dominated. The biggest male member of the group could do whatever he wanted. He could take for himself the most food and the best food. He could take for himself the most women and the best women. He could physically overcome anybody who opposed him.

But there was one limitation. A limitation that did not

apply to males not living in groups. They could be completely dominant. The limitation for the human alpha male was that he needed the other males to help defend the group. Even the strongest male could be overcome by numbers. So, while a single male could dominate the group, he could not totally disregard the other males. Or the leftover females they could have sex with. He had to leave something for them.

Chapter 6

Democracy became the prevailing form of government and mental capacity gained on physical capacity.

Human groups in the later primitive age were made up of a small number of males and the females and children they could protect and provide for. They had reached this size because some human beings, with their limited thinking, had realized they could live together in such numbers. Once that was realized, all had to live together in larger numbers to survive. Because the capacity to defend themselves and attack others depended upon numbers.

The size of the groups was determined by the area they could defend and how much food they could find there. Given what they ate and how they got it, this was not much. Groups remained small.

The same thinking that caused the larger groups ended the dominance of a single male. This was that numbers, not individual physical capacity, determined strength.

The males in a group could combine and overcome any single male who tried to dominate them. This made democracy the prevailing form of government.

With democracy mental capacity gained on physical capacity. It was no longer the physical capacity of a single male that determined group behavior. All males contributed. What seemed the best thing to do to the majority was what was done.

Mental capacity had more and more effect as language developed. Because more could be dealt with with language. And it was largely through language that mental capacity could be shown.

Chapter 7

The agricultural age was a dark age for mental capacity.

Chapter 8

The agricultural age was a dark age for mental capacity because it ended democracy.

Minority rule replaced majority rule. Because an organized minority could dominate an unorganized majority. The gains for mental capacity that came with democracy were lost.

Actually, the uses to which mental capacity could be put increased. Life was far more complicated in the agricultural age than in the primitive age. There were means for doing things besides simply subsist. But this new situation was taken advantage of only unintentionally and on a very small scale. The rule minorities were interested in war, not production. They achieved and held their special position through war. They thought of production as beneath them. They knew their military strength depended on production, but they did not know production could be increased through the use of mental capacity. They thought the methods of production in their time were the only methods of production. And because they thought this they did nothing to try to improve those methods.

Chapter 9

The agricultural age was a dark age for mental capacity because it brought inequality and inheritance.

Human beings lived in equality during the primitive age. Everything in their lives was open to them. Whatever capacity they had, whether mental or physical, could be put to use. They could benefit from it. The human beings they lived with could benefit from it.

The agricultural age brought inequality because it ended collectives. Areas were divide dup. Families became responsible for their own members. The inequality that resulted gave some human beings more opportunity than others.

This situation could have ended when a generation died off. The next generation could have started all over again. But that did not happen. Inheritance was introduced. Families kept whatever earlier generations had acquired. And added to it when they could. Inequality remained. It grew greater.

Family members had to marry outside their own family. This combined inheritances. They could get bigger and bigger as marriages continued generation after generation.

What anyone could accomplish depended not only on his personal qualities but on the means at his disposal and his relations with other human beings. Those who got inheritances benefited from both the means and the relations. So much so that their personal qualities could matter very little.

That was all the more so because of the stability of the system. Inheritances could and did stay in the same families century after century. Those who benefited could be incompetent or worse. They did not lose their positions. Infighting in the ruling minorities sometimes caused a few changes. But, generally, lack of personal qualities had no serious unfavorable consequences.

This meant there was little or no competition at the higher levels. And where there is no competition there is no inducement or compulsion to use mental capacity. Evolution works because of competition. Competition produces innovation and adaptation. So more can be gotten out of an environment. This was happening only minimally during the agricultural age.

Chapter 10

The agricultural age was a dark age for mental capacity because it caused kingship.

With kingship, which was hereditary, mental capacity had no bearing on who exercised the highest authority in a country. Whoever it was could be totally unqualified. Even though kingdoms competed. Which could seem to mean they had to pick the best leaders to survive. But despite this kingship was the prevailing form of government throughout the thousands of years of the agricultural age.

The explanation is simple. Kings were bad but they were the least bad alternative for countries. Without kings there would have been struggles within the ruling minorities for supreme leadership whenever a supreme leader had to be chosen. These struggles would have weakened those countries. A neighboring country or a combination of neighboring countries could then have defeated them and taken them over.

There was a contributing factor. Members of ruling minorities found it natural for inheritance to determine position. That was their system. That was what they owed their own position to. But what worked not too badly on the lower levels did not on the highest level. Kings had more than serfs and crops to deal with. Their mistakes involved whole countries. But the need for unity overrode all else. Many royal houses lasted for centuries.

Chapter 11

The ruling minorities of the agricultural age were so taken up with self-glorification they had practically no appreciation of mental capacity.

Their overriding interest was to get more for themselves. But the only way they could think of doing that was through getting more of what was available by taking it from others. It never occurred to them that another way would be to increase what was available.

There were excuses for this.

Innovation happened rarely in the agricultural age. Generations could pass without any. And there was no knowledge of how or where earlier innovation had taken place. As far as members of the ruling minorities were concerned, methods and means of production had always been the same. Had they had any knowledge of history, they might have thought differently. But they did not. What passed for history for them was a small collection of stories about members of their class. Which contributed nothing to practical thinking about production.

The rule of the ruling minorities was absolute. There were no limitations on their power. This led them to treat other members of their society however they wanted. Which turned out to be that they exploited, oppressed and humiliated them. The only ones who might get occasional benign treatment from them were those who served them loyally.

The behavior the ruling minorities forced on those below them added to the contempt they already felt because of the difference in position. And the conditions those below them lived in—because of the exactions of the ruling minorities—further added to their contempt.

While the ruling minorities were thinking of their inferiors with contempt, they were thinking of themselves as the finest of human beings. Their favorite pastime was listening to themselves be praised. This pastime was institutionalized in all their societies. None was without story tellers whose job was to praise the powerful in the most extravagant terms imaginable.

Actually, the range among human beings is not that great. As the modern age eventually demonstrated, when the lower classes were given opportunities and produced outstanding successes in all activities. And the upper classes, despite all the advantages they still enjoyed, made a much poorer showing than might have been expected. So the thousands of years of the agricultural age was proved to have been based on a false theory of humanity. A very pervasive, generally accepted false theory.

Chapter 12

Gunpowder and printing jointly caused the Industrial Revolution.

Gunpowder because it provided much of the wealth needed to increase production.

Printing because it caused the sharing of knowledge needed to increase production.

Gunpowder here means both gunpowder and the means of effectively using it in war. Gunpowder by itself would have accomplished little or nothing. The Chinese discovered gunpowder, but did not get much advantage out of it because they did not also discover effective means of using it.

The means of effectively using gunpowder were not already available. And it took a long time to come up with them. It was not until the 15th century that the means were effective enough so that gunpowder really mattered. And once that stage had been reached further discoveries were made. And are still being made now.

Europe was able to conquer the world with gunpowder. It was that superior to other forms of weapons. And not only was Europe able to conquer the world. It could do that with very little manpower. Which was critical. At the time Europe did not have enough excess manpower to conquer the world unless it could do so with a small minority of its people.

The conquest of the world enabled Europe to loot and exploit. And while much of the wealth that resulted went into unproductive uses, much of it was used in production. Europe itself at the time was creating some wealth, but not nearly enough to finance first its enormous increase in trade and then the Industrial Revolution.

The looting and exploitation Europe did was not unusual. Once it became possible, as it did with agriculture, looting and exploitation happened all the time because it was the cheapest way to get wealth. Wealth had to be created through production, but once wealth was created it could be appropriated. Appropriating it did not cost as much as creating it, so appropriating it ws preferred.

War not only made appropriation possible. It mad exploitation possible. Because those who won in war could make those who lost do whatever they wanted. Which included working involuntarily and not getting paid according to how much they produced.

European conquest differed because it sometimes combined looting and exploitation with contributing to production.

All peoples think of the area they live in as their own. They think everything in it belongs to them. So they think when foreigners come in and use some of that area in production, those foreigners are stealing from them.

This can be either true or false, depending on the circumstances. It is an argument that needs qualification.

No people owns an area in the sense that it was always theirs. All areas have been taken from the previous inhabitants. No people today has an original ownership claim.

As to foreigners stealing from the current inhabitants of an area. A case can be made for this if foreigners just come in and loot and exploit. But the Europeans did not always do only this. And they did less of it as time went by. Europeans sometimes added to production because they brought in better methods of production. And Europeans sometimes added to production because they used their own wealth to increase production.

When Europeans used their own wealth to increase the means of production, the local inhabitants benefited. They got jobs—jobs that otherwise would not have existed. The Europeans did not have enough excess manpower to fill all the jobs they created. The same lack of manpower that made gunpowder decisive for them forced them to benefit the local inhabitants of the countries they conquered by providing them jobs.

Both gunpowder and printing became big factors in the later part of the 15th century.

Printing caused knowledge to be shared on a much larger scale. Printing is far cheaper than writing. So it is far more accessible. It spreads more knowledge than writing alone possibly could.

Europe was lucky in that printing got a big boost from a special situation which existed at the time. This was the break-up of the Catholic Church. The Protestants made their version of Christianity depend on knowledge of the Bible. This provided a large market for the Bible shortly after the invention of a practical method of printing.

Protestants did not only want a Bible. They had to be able to read if they were going to read that Bible. And once they were able to read the Bible they could read anything else that was printed.

With gunpowder and printing Europe was on its way. First it set out on conquest. Then it produced the Industrial Revolution.

Chapter 13

With the Industrial Revolution mental capacity triumphed over physical capacity.

Language made this triumph possible. But only under the right circumstances. The Industrial Revolution finally provided the right circumstances.

Chapter 14

The Industrial Revolution steadily increased the number of workers doing mental work compared to the number of workers doing physical work.

In the agricultural age very few workers did mental work. Throughout the world—in the parts dependent on agriculture—the overwhelming majority of the populations did physical work. Because agriculture at the time consisted almost entirely of physical work. There was some mental work in towns and cities, but it was infinitesimal compared to physical work. To start with, towns and cities were rare even in the parts of t he world where they existed, and during some periods they were next to non-existent. And even when they were at their most numerous almost all of the work done in them had to be physical because there was no alternative. The machines that took over physical work had not been invented.

The great idea behind the Industrial Revolution was that work could be done by machines. Not by human beings, not by animals, but by machines. The machines at first replaced physical work. Eventually they came to replace much mental work as well.

In both cases the replacement was only partial. Some of the physical work still had to be left to human beings and animals. Some of the mental work still had to be left to human beings. Machines had to be thought up and designed.

They did not create themselves like living creatures. And machines had to be tended and repaired. They could not work indefinitely on their own. But the physical work that remained for human beings was very much less than the physical work that was once required. And the mental work required from human beings was greatly increased. So the ratio between the two changed drastically.

Chapter 15

The Industrial Revolution brought back the conditions on which evolution depends.

These conditions are competition and innovation.

During the agricultural age the human species repressed both competition and innovation. The repression was largely successful. There was little of either during thousands of years.

Human beings do not like competition or innovation. Competition and innovation make life difficult for all creatures. Often so much so that they die. They would much prefer to do without them. But the other creatures have no choice. Evolution imposes competition and innovation on them. Evolution would not work without them.

The only creatures that like innovation are those that benefit from it. Either they embody it themselves or something in their environment embodies it. But most innovation in nature are not beneficial. They are experiments that do not work. And the innovations that are beneficial to some creatures are not to the others that do not embody it themselves or have it embodies in something in their environment. So most innovations have not been beneficial to a majority of the creatures they affected.

For human beings in the agricultural age innovation was something they could control. In this they became different from other creatures. In the primitive age they had been like

83

other creatures in the beginning. Nature imposed innovation on them through heredity. Then, as their intelligence developed, they began providing some of the innovation themselves. By the time of the agricultural age they were providing all of the innovation themselves. They stopped evolving through heredity.

While human beings benefited from innovation in general, they were likely to oppose and repress specific innovations. At the beginning an innovation benefited only one or a few of those with the knowledge the innovation consisted of. Those without that knowledge were put at a disadvantage if those with the innovation competed with them. They could overcome the disadvantage they were put at only if they could acquire the innovation themselves. Which they might or might not be able to do. But even if they could acquire it themselves, they might be opposed to doing that because they would then make some of their previous methods and tools worthless.

During the agricultural age human beings were usually able to limit competition and innovation because of how they lived.

Their communities were small and difficult to reach. Those within communities could prevent products from outside coming in. Besides which transportation was so expensive and slow that products from outside usually would cost more than local products. The result was that only products that were not produced locally would get in.

Within communities producers maintained monopolies for themselves. This was easy for them to do. Their customers were in no position to force them to compete. And they did not want to compete because they could make more money without competition.

The monopolies enabled them to stifle innovation. They were the only ones who could put innovation to use. They did not choose to because they made money with the known methods and products. They saw nothing to gain from the disruption innovation would cause.

Then the Industrial Revolution forced competition and innovation on human beings.

Because of advances in transportation communities could compete with one another. That protection from competition they had enjoyed was gone.

The Industrial Revolution made the scale of production much greater. Machines were used. Machines that provided power the like of which had never been known before. Products had been produced one at a time. Or a few at a time. With machines products were being produced in large numbers. They could not all be sold in the communities where they were produced. A percentage of them had to be transported and sold elsewhere. Which meant that other communities had to let them in. And did let them in because they were so much cheaper. It was no longer a matter of underselling local production by some small margin. It was a matter of underselling local production by so much that local production could not be monopolized.

The advent of competition opened up the world to innovation. Producers wanted to produce more cheaply so they could sell more. Innovation enabled them to sell more cheaply with more efficient means of production. And innovation enabled them to sell products they had never sold before. Products that without innovation would not have existed.

And innovation was possible because knowledge was being shared. The more information that accumulated, the more innovation became possible. And the more innovation was sought. Because money could be made from innovation. Much money. Not only from thinking it up. But from applying it.

Chapter 16

But while the Industrial Revolution brought back competition and innovation, it eventually provided the means for limiting them.

The Industrial Revolution made strong central governments possible. Strong central governments could limit competition and innovation.

The Industrial Revolution made strong central governments possible because it provided the means to exercise authority. Before the Industrial Revolution central governments were weak. Though they seemed strong at the time because they were strong compared to the governments that preceded them. These seemingly strong governments had to rely on hierarchies to enforce their authority. They could not do that themselves. They did not know enough about what was going on outside their immediate vicinity. They could not get their distant subordinates to obey them. Those subordinates were close to autonomous. They could do what benefited them. And did. Royal authority was more of an illusion than than a reality.

The Industrial Revolution provided central governments with the means of knowing what was going on throughout their countries. And the means of giving orders to deal with whatever that was. Orders that arrived quickly. Subordinates lost most of their autonomy. And central governments acquired the means of enforcing their authority. They had national armies and national legal systems. Both essential elements for making central governments effective. They were no longer dependent on enforcement from below. The conditions that made for local autonomy were gone.

The Industrial Revolution only gradually provided the means for central governments to exercise their authority. It was during that interim period that competition and innovation thrived.

Chapter 17

The Great Depression caused the welfare state.

The welfare state, logically, should have happened much sooner than it did. Democracy was introduced in the late 18th century. By the late 19th century it prevailed not only in the United States but in other parts of the world, including Great Britain and France. It spread further in the 20th century.

Democracy, logically, should have quickly produced the welfare state. The majorities in democracies were not well-off. More importantly, they did not have security. Capitalism, the economic system in democracies, did not provide security. The majorities could have used their votes to change the system, turning it into the welfare state. They had the numbers. Then they would have been better-off and they would have had more security.

This did not happen.

Countries' attitudes are hard to change. Human beings are taught their attitudes when they are growing up. They are too young to think. So their attitudes are not thought out. Normally, they go through life with them. It takes a big change in conditions to make their attitudes change. A big enough change to make the attitudes they were taught to become unsuitable.

Human beings had had more or less the same attitudes throughout the agricultural age. These were the attitudes suitable to states that were not welfare states. Governments were not responsible for families. Families were responsible for themselves.

The Industrial Revolution did not change this situation. Families continued to be responsible for themselves. They might be helped by others through charity. But charity was voluntary and limited. It never provided for all those who needed it.

The Industrial Revolution brought democracy.

Democracy made it possible for majorities to introduce the welfare state. But the old attitudes persisted. Families were still able—most of the time—to look after their own. Members were still living from agriculture. They could look after others in need. There were bad periods. But they did not last that along. They did not affect that many. The old attitudes remained.

Then the Great Depression happened. World War I had already weakened old attitudes. There was a greater readiness to make changes. The Great Depression provided the occasion. It lasted a long time. It affected large numbers. The old responses were not sufficient. Governments had to start interfering in their economics. They had to provide help. They had to provide jobs. Families could not be left to themselves.

And businesses could not be left to themselves. They were not recovering. They, too, needed help. They needed government intervention. Families could not be helped unless businesses were helped, since businesses provided the jobs.

By the time World War II started, the principle of government intervention was established. The old self-reliance of families, of business had been left behind.

Once the principle of government intervention was established, government intervention could only increase. Money could be gotten from it. So money—more and more—was spent to get it. And more and more votes were cast to get it. The welfare state had arrived.

Chapter 18

Competition and innovation are two ways of increasing production. They get different treatments.

Competition works by getting the most out of what is available for production. Innovation works by increasing the capacity of production that already exists or creating new production.

Central governments can control how much competition and innovation happen in their countries. They have the means.

Communist governments allowed only minimal competition. Because competition would have made them give their populations what those populations wanted. And they, the communist governments, wanted to give those populations what they wanted to give them. Which then allowed the governments to provide more for other purposes that were more important for them.

Communist governments allowed only selective innovation. They did not allow innovation that made existing facilities obsolete. Because that would not have been in their interest. The exception was military production. Here·they had to compete with other countries. So they had to accept innovation.

Democratic governments started out by allowing both competition and innovation. That was what maximized production. But they ran into competition.

Workers did not like competition because it kept their wages down to how much they produced. Businesses did not like competition because it kept their profits down by making them lower prices. Workers formed unions and limited competition. They raised their wages above where productivity would have put them. Businesses engaged in practices that limited competition. They raised their prices above where competition would have put them.

Workers and businesses had opposed innovation before the Industrial Revolution. They both had monopolies. They did not want to lose them. Which was what innovation threatened to make happen.

With the coming of the Industrial Revolution innovation changed its nature. It had meant changes with relatively small-scale results. So long as the amount of power remained the same, this was bound to be so. When innovation revolutionized power with the steam engine, the results of innovation became large-scale. So large-scale that resistance was overwhelmed. Neither workers nor businesses could stop the new methods and the new products.

Steam power carried other innovations with it. The increase in production raised standards of living.

Workers with innovation produced more than workers without innovation. The increase in production was measured as in increase in workers' productivity. But it was not that. Workers by themselves were not able to produce more. The increase was caused by innovation, not by workers.

With the welfare state democratic governments limited competition. They interfered in economic matters to prevent production from being distributed according to contribution to production. They made favored workers and businesses get more than they would have through competition. But these governments, unlike communist governments, did not limit innovation. Because they realized that innovation was the principal cause of increased production. And their populations, and so the governments themselves, wanted increased production. Innovation was a gift. An endless gift.

Chapter 19

The expansion of knowledge that started with the second kind of consciousness has finally brought human beings as close to paradise as they are going to get.

With the second kind of consciousness human beings could think. Thinking led to speech. Speech led to sharing knowledge. Sharing knowledge led to innovation. Innovation increased production. There is no limit on how much it can do this. What seems prodigious now could be only the beginning. Plenty is possible. Plenty for all. Which is as close to paradise as the human species can get.

VIII.

Why The Great Religions Were All Mistaken About Morality

Chapter 1

The great religions were all mistaken about morality. Modern times have demonstrated that.

The great religions believed that morality had to be combined with rewards and punishments provided by God. In the West these rewards and punishments came in an other world for the dead. In the East they came in this world through reincarnation.

The great religious arrived at their beliefs because they saw morality was not rewarded and punished appropriately in this world. So, if morality was to be observed, this shortcoming had to be made up for. Otherwise, they thought, human beings would not behave morally.

But modern times have demonstrated that morality is both believed in and practiced without the great religions and their systems of rewards and punishments. Human beings who no longer believe in the great religions still believe in morality.

Chapter 2

What the great religions did not realize was that childhood gives human beings a belief in morality that stays with them all their lives whether they believe in God and religion or not.

Children have to be taught morality so they will behave properly. Human beings, unlike most creatures, are not born with all the behavior they need. Of all species they are the one most in need of training. That is what makes for their adaptability.

Children have to be taught a simple morality. They are not old enough to be trained any other way. Their intelligence would not be up to it.

They are told this is good and that is bad. They are

John Weyland

encouraged to do what is good and discouraged from doing what is bad. The adults who raise them have enough control over them to do this.

Children grow up thinking good and bad exist. That is easily explicable. What is not so easily explicable is why they continue when they are older to think good and bad exist. With their adult intelligence they can understand that good and bad are what they are: concepts necessary for training the young. But they also should be able to see they are just that and nothing more. But they do not.

Other beliefs have been rejected, including the belief in God. In the more advanced parts of the world the belief in God has become an anachronism. Human beings have shown themselves capable of seeing it for what it is. They should realize that the belief in the existence of good and bad is dependent on the belief in God and should be rejected along with it. But this has not happened.

Chapter 3

Morality is dependent on the belief in God because only the belief in God can give morality an independent existence.

Morality has to be defined. What is good? What is bad? Only God can define morality. Otherwise it is just a matter of opinion. And no particular opinion has to be accepted.

During the long period when God was believed in this dependence or morality did not pose a problem. Everybody believed in God. Part of the belief in God was that he defined morality. Morality was what God said it was. This gave morality an independent existence. What it was could be known and had to be accepted. It was not just a matter of opinion.

When the belief in god began to be questioned, the dependence of morality on this belief was not realized.

Human beings were so used to accepting the independent existence of morality that they did not realize it was being undermined. They thought they knew what morality was.

Their certainty was so great there were no disputes. Morality was to continue without any dependence on the belief in God. Human beings were so used to believing in it they could not imagine a world in which it did not exist.

Chapter 4

Without God morality cannot be reasoned about.

All the reasoning about morality is futile unless morality has an independent existence.

Morality is what anybody wants it to be. And nobody can force anybody else to accept his definition.

Some human beings can accept the same definition of morality. They can be powerful enough to make their definition the legal definition. They can get it enforced. But this does not compel those who disagree with them to accept that definition. They can abide by it because it is the legal definition. And what is illegal is punished. But they do not have to believe in it.

There is a naive belief in democracies that everybody has to accept the will of the majority. That this is so because of some form of logic. But this is to confuse law and morality. Everybody does have to accept the will of the majority when it is expressed in law. Or risk punishment. But everybody does not have to accept the reasoning supporting that will of the majority. Because there is no reasoning that can support morality. It is not just this reasoning or that reasoning is wrong. All reasoning to support morality is wrong. Just as all reasoning against morality is wrong. Morality cannot be proved or disproved by reasoning. To think that it can be is to show a refusal to think.

Chapter 5

The practical effects of morality can be reasoned about.

Morality was chosen from the beginning for its practical effects. It is only that it existed so long that it was thought to have some other quality.

Sexual morality is a good example. Once the agricultural age started women and children had to be supported by individual men. They were going to support only the women and children who belonged to them. That meant chastity in girls and faithfulness in wives. And, to a large extent, chastity in boys and faithfulness in men because there were no girls or women to be unchaste with. (Except, later on, prostitutes, and there were not many of them.) Homosexuality was forbidden. Numbers were needed to fight wars and do work. Homosexuality did not produce numbers.

All other morality was likewise chosen for its practical effects. Just as laws were chosen for their practical effects.

With the coming of the Industrial Revolution human society changed. It was not just that more was produced because of machines.

The Industrial Revolution brought democracy.

There had been minority rule during the agricultural age. The morality that was chosen was the morality that suited the majority. With democracy changes had to be made in morality if it was to suit the majority.

And the Industrial Revolution brought independence for women. It gave them jobs outside the home. They no longer had to be supported by men. So more changes in morality had to be made if it was to suit independent women. Who not only became economically independent but politically equal.

The sensible way to deal with the new situation would have been to determine the practical effects and make changes in morality accordingly. Instead there was useless and endless controversy about what was right.

Chapter 6

What can happen when the practical effects of morality are disregarded is demonstrated by unmarried mothers.

Birth control pills made promiscuity for women practical. It had been the risk of pregnancy that had caused it to be impractically throughout the late agricultural age.

So it was decided women had a right to be promiscuous. It was assumed they would not become pregnant. Of if they did become pregnant they would have an abortion.

Giving birth to children outside of marriage had always been condemned. Women who had children like that became outcasts. They were given no help. Which they usually needed, since they had no means of earning a living.

But the assumption about women not becoming pregnant turned out to be false. The welfare state had been established. All who needed help got help. Including unmarried mothers. For many women this turned out to be decisive. They preferred being unmarried and independent to being married. So they got pregnant when they could have avoided getting pregnant and they did not have an abortion when they could have gotten an abortion.

The many women who preferred being unmarried mothers proved to be millions in welfare countries. The government help was enough to keep them and their child (or children) alive. But, even if they did work, not enough to enable them to live as well as married couple.

There are bad results. The general populations of the countries where these women live have to support them and their children. And the children get an unsatisfactory childhood and a poorer adult life.

Chapter 7

Morality is used to force beliefs on others.

An essential part of the meaning of morality is that it should be obeyed. Like the orders of parents to their children. Children are to do what they are told.

Those who make pronouncements on morality take it upon themselves to determine what should be done. They arrogate that power to themselves. Which they believe they are fully entitled to do. They are convinced they know what is right. And because of that what they say should be accepted.

They never have misgivings because they never question the nature of morality. They consider that self-evident. It is what they take it to be. They are dictating to others, not reasoning with them. Though they pretend to do that. It is only a pretense because the conclusion is a foregone conclusion. Not only a foregone conclusion, but the only possible conclusion. So whatever reasoning takes place is unavoidably futile.

Chapter 8

Morality is used to invent rights.

Rights were invented for use against monarchies. Their purpose was to justify limitations on monarchs' powers.

These rights were called natural rights. That rights exist in nature is nonsense. The natural rights philosophy achieved popularity because it could be used to oppose the divine rights philosophy of monarchies.

The American and French revolutions gave natural rights respectability because they were crucial to their justification. That allowed the publics in both countries to take them seriously after they passed out of favor in philosophy itself.

Their usefulness for later changes in morality has been

exploited. The union movement discovered that workers have rights. Other rights were discovered as the welfare state was adopted and the sexual revolution took place.

The process for establishing rights starts out with the assertion that they exist. Then it goes on to getting them turned into law. There really are rights in law. They are enforceable. So while at the beginning of the assertion of rights is false, it can be made true.

Chapter 9

Rights are actually determined by pressure groups and money.

They do not necessarily represent majority thinking. Majority thinking itself can be opposed to them.

Morality used to be determined by religions. They were the only organizations with regular access to the public. So only they could determine morality.

Religions did not tolerate dissent. They punished it. Those who did not accept their morality kept quiet. Or risked punishment, including death. So the degree of rejection was never known.

Religious still exist, but they no longer exert the authority they used to. Their power is the vestige of their former power. Their place has been taken by the media. It is pressure groups and money that have access to the media. The attitudes the public see and hear there make up their morality. They have nowhere else to get it from.

Their public attitude, that is. Their private attitude can be different.

Not very many members of the public are ready to speak out against the prescribed morality. They know that this would bring down condemnation on them. And even if they are ready to speak out they are not given access to the media. So their dissent remains private.

The pressure groups and the money do not use the same means of enforcement as the religions did. They do not have to. They have established a code for what can be said and what cannot be said. Those who violate that code are banned. They no longer have access to the media.

Token dissent is allowed. But the basic attitudes of the new morality have to be respected. Which in effect endorses them.

Behind all of those basic attitudes is the assumption that morality exists. So all discussions of morality are nonsense. What passes for morality is what is supported by pressure groups and money. There is nothing more to it than that.

IX.

Why The Individual
Voter Is Powerless

Chapter 1

Individuals are politically helpless in modern democracies.

Chapter 2

Because individuals are politically helpless in modern democracies, they are wasting their time if they behave like model citizens.

They are wasting their time if they try to understand the political issues. They are wasting their time if they actively support this or that candidate. They are wasting their time if they vote or otherwise take part in any political activity.

Chapter 3

If individuals recognized their political helplessness, modern democracies would not work.

Modern democracies work only because individuals believe they are not politically helpless and so take part in voting and other political activities.

Some of them. The rate of participation is high enough to support the illusion that the accepted view if the correct view. Those who do not vote or otherwise participate do not because of lack of interest and laziness. It is not because they have seen through the system.

Chapter 4

Individuals are taught that their vote counts and other accepted beliefs about political participation.

Children are not critical. They do not have the experience that would enable them to be. They believe what they are told by persons in authority. Like their parents. Like their teachers. What they are told is the orthodoxy of modern democracies.

When children get older, they have more experience and become capable of being critical. They can then become receptive to beliefs different from those they were told they should have. These can include many that are critical of contemporary conditions in modern democracies. But they do not include any that challenge how voting works.

Left to themselves, individuals hesitate to reject accepted beliefs. They are not that confidant of their ability to deal with evidence and logic. It is one thing when alternative beliefs are involved that have much support. That gives them confidence. It is another thing when they have only their own ability and experience to go by.

A good example is: "Your vote does not count." This is a simple statement. It is unquestionably backed by logic and evidence. But it rejected by authority. And it is rejected by the general public. So there is hesitancy about accepting it. If not outright refusal.

Other similar statements about political participation are treated similarly. Being true does not guarantee their acceptance.

Chapter 5

Individuals are conditioned by their childhood experience to believe their vote counts.

Childhood experience has to do with small groups. Family, relatives, friends, neighbors, class, teams, gangs, etc. The individual does count in small groups. Being for or against something can be decisive. Even when not decisive it can matter. It can influence others. And the individual is treated accordingly. The individual has some control over what is done.

This small group experience continues on a limited scale after childhood. It can happen at colleges. It can happen at work. It can happen in local organizations. It can keep happening throughout life.

But it does not happen when how a country is run is being determined. Or when how the bigger parts of that country are run is being determined. Then large groups are involved. And large groups work differently than small groups.

This is not part of generally shared knowledge. It is not a subject that gets public attention. Because such knowledge would undermine democracy.

Luckily for democracy, almost all individuals let their childhood experience, and the follow-up to that experience in later life, determine their thinking. They accept the illusion of democracy. They ignore the reality.

Chapter 6

Individuals have no effective access to the public by which they could offset their political helplessness.

Effective access used to be through churches. They had a monopoly on access to the public. Then it became through churches, books, newspaper and magazines. Then radio and television were added. But individuals had no access to these media.

Finally, the internet did provide individuals with access. But it is access the public largely ignores. Experience has shown this offers little or nothing to most individuals. They do not have the time or inclination to use it. And when they do their use seldom has much effect. It just gets no attention. They are left with their single vote.

Whether a single vote has any effect depends upon the total of votes involved. It certainly can if that total is 50 or less. The likelihood becomes smaller the closer the total gets to the higher end. After 50 the likelihood becomes very slight. After 100, extremely slight. After 200 or so, non-existent. And very few elections involve fewer than 200 votes. In most elections more votes are involved and the possibility of a single vote deciding the outcome is nil.

Chapter 7

For most of their existence human beings did live in a situation where their vote counted.

This was during the primitive age. In the primitive age human beings lived in small groups. Which were run democratically, because the majority was stronger than a minority and could prevail. They had no problem with access, since they lived together.

With the agricultural age human beings started living in larger groups. These larger groups made real democracy impossible. Their members could not come together to make democratic decisions. But that was irrelevant. The larger groups were run by minorities, since through organization they could concentrate their numbers and so dominate the majorities, which were dispersed and had no organization.

The rare and so-called democracies of the agricultural age were not real democracies. They were towns with surrounding countrysides. Only the townsmen could meet regularly, which left out the countrymen. And even the townsmen could not meet often enough to actually run their governments. They had to delegate authority to representatives. And if history has shown anything it has shown delegated authority is lost authority. Those exercising it cannot be completely controlled. The townsmen did retain some authority, but it was to approve or disapprove at intervals one act or or a few acts of their representatives. And the numbers involved were so large that single votes could not count.

When so-called democracy reappeared in the modern age, it was like the few and short-lived democracies of the agricultural age. Except that it was even more representative and less democratic. The situation of the primitive age did not reoccur.

Chapter 8

It is harder for individuals to accept their political helplessness because they encourage one another to think they matter politically.

They exchange political opinions. They urge one another to keep up with current events. They favor taking part in political activities. That all gives them a feeling of political importance.

Individuals have always had opinions about political matters. Since those matters affect their lives. But with the advent of the agricultural age and civilization the expression of political opinions was restricted. There was minority rule. The minorities exploited and oppressed the majorities. They forbade the expression of political opinions critical of themselves and their rule. Those opinions might be expressed with family members and friends, but great caution had to be exercised even then, for fear that reports of what they were saying would get out.

With democracy the situation is different. Individuals can express their political opinions. Which gives the illusion that those opinions matter. Which in turn encourages individuals to express those opinions. But the system does not work as it seems to. Only organized numbers and money count.

Proof of this is that poll numbers are routinely disregarded when they go against organized numbers and money.

Chapter 9

Advice to individuals to get involved in the system if they want to change it is bad advice. The system will change them. They will not change the system.

The system is essentially the same in all democracies in advanced countries. It is the same because conditions in those countries necessarily cause just one system to exist. No other system is possible.

Chapter 10

The system in democracies in advanced countries is a system of open bribery.

This is a relatively new system. Bribery has always existed. But it used to be hidden bribery.

Hidden bribery still goes on. It is illegal but it is hard to prove. Usually it can only be suspected.

Hidden bribery is only a small part of the bribery in advanced countries. There is little need for it. Since open bribery is available. And open bribery is legal.

Open bribery is campaign contributions. It is given for the same reason as hidden bribery: to get politicians to do something or not to do something. But it is not given to the politicians themselves. It is given to their campaigns. Without which they could not continue to be politicians.

Open bribery did not always exist like hidden bribery. It did not always exist because campaigns did not always exist. Campaigns came in with democracy. Once campaigns came in open bribery started.

But open bribery used not to occur on such a large scale. This was for two reasons. Until the 20th century campaigns were not that expensive. And until the 20th century governments did not have that much to sell.

Campaigns became so expensive because the means

of conducting them became so expensive. Politicians needed much more money for campaigns than before. And campaigns became so expensive because the value of what could be bought through campaign contributions increased so much. Politicians could demand much more than before. And politicians had to demand much more than before.

Chapter 10

Governments have so much to sell because they do so much they used not to do.

They are thought of as giving out money. Which they do a lot of. And which causes a large part of campaign contributions. But another large part is caused by their control of what goes on in their countries.

Governments used to control very little of what went on in their countries. They were not expected to. Then in the 20th century they started controlling more and more.

The thinking was that government control would prevent what should not happen from happening. It seemed so simple. Things supposedly were happening in ways they should not be happening. Have governments intervene. With laws and regulations and regulatory agencies they could insure that only what should happen did happen.

Only the politically sophisticated realized that more laws and more regulations would cause more bribery. Those affected by the laws would want laws favorable to them. Those being regulated would want regulations favorable to them. They would be willing to pay to get the favorable laws and regulations. So they would pay more to the politicians in charge of passing the laws and making the regulations.

Those being regulated would also want regulatory agencies favorable to them. Bribing the members would have been the old-fashioned method that would have been used. But that would have been illegal and possibly counter-productive. The new method was to make the members of the regulatory agencies want to please those being regulated. This was easy to do. Those in the regulatory agencies had to understand both the regulations and the activities they applied to. That meant when they worked in the activities they were qualified to work in the agencies. So they went back and forth. They had no competition, since nobody else had their qualifications. The higher they rose in the agency, the higher they would rise in the activity. And vice versa. And the more they made. It was a mutually satisfactory arrangement. It was not open bribery, but it served the same purpose.

Chapter 12

The founders of democracy did not foresee the problems of democracy with voting.

Those who founded democracies thought voting would be a simple manner. The qualified voters in a certain area would vote. There would be a majority for something or against something. That would decide the issue. The majority would prevail.

They knew they were introducing a representative and not a democratic system, since a democratives system was not possible with the large areas and numbers involved. But they did not see this having any consequences they really had to concern themselves with.

Because of that they did not foresee that organizations would have to develop to turn powerless individual voters into powerful blocs of voters.

The first such organizations were political parties. Political parties had different programs, so voters could groups according to which programs they favored.

Political parties not not really give individuals any new power. But they did enable them to think they were serving causes they believed in by voting for their party's candidates.

This encouraged them to vote, while logically as individuals they were just as powerless as before.

Political parties also had benefits to bestow, so they could reward those who served them. That enabled them to maintain their organizations.

Special groups representing special causes could also appeal to blocs of voters. But they usually operated through the parties.

The big change came with the interventionist state. Then, because there was so much to gain, the special groups came to operate largely on their own. As did businesses, which had their particular interests along with the interests of business in general.

The special groups could offer both votes and money. Businesses had their own money. Special groups raised money from their members. But they also had votes, which businesses did not. It took a combination of the two to win elections, so politicians had to have support from both. How much of one and how much of the other varied from election to election, and nobody knew for sure just what would work. But one thing was sure. The bigger government became, the more important money became because the more government had for sale. That is why the amounts of money spent on politics keep increasing.

Chapter 13

There are alternatives to the present system. But they will not be adopted because they would not be supported by the forces which now control voting.

The alternatives are:

Compulsory voting.

Electronic voting, which would allow all voters to vote instead of representatives.

Real limits on campaign contributions.

Chapter 14

Compulsory voting would solve the logical problem of voting but it would not solve the powerless voter problem.

Compulsory voting would make voters vote even if they knew their vote was useless.

But compulsory voting would not give individual voters any more power. Their single vote still would not decide anything.

The forces which now control voting do not want compulsory voting. They are satisfied with the present system, since it works to their advantage. They are afraid compulsory would produce different results.

But this has not happened where compulsory voting has been tried. The voters who have been forced to turn out have shown themselves to be very like the voters who have turned out voluntarily. So the fear that they would produce different results might be groundless. But the thinking of the forces which now control voting is: Why take a chance?

Besides which, getting to more voters would cost more money. Why spend more money?

Chapter 15

Electronic voting would make real democracy possible.

Real democracy is now possible with large, dispersed populations when it had always been impossible before. With the new technology all voters could be asked to vote every day, or however often was necessary for them to vote on all the legislation considered by their legislatures. This would be practical.

Voting could be voluntary or compulsory.

Representative government would then be made an anachronism. All of its disadvantages could be things of the past.

But the forces which now control voting do not want electronic voting. They would not be able to use open bribery with whole populations. And it is open bribery which allows them to buy exactly what they want.

Pressure groups and businesses could try to use money to determine the results of electronic voting. But the cost of doing this would be much greater. And the outcomes would be much more uncertain. With the present system they can buy politicians long-term. Because those politicians know they are going to need future contributions. So long as they remain politicians. And those future contributions are going to have to come from the same sources as present contributions. In short, they can be bought and they will stay bought.

The general public is different. Through commercials they can be persuaded to be for this and against that. They can be bought. But they cannot be made to stay bought. New persuasion would have to be used each time legislation came up. And that would be frequently.

This persuasion would have to be complicated, whereas now it is simple. The pressure groups and businesses tell the politicians to vote for this or vote against that. They do. No other persuasion is needed but the open bribery. With electronic voting the persuasion that would work would be much more difficult to determine. There is no science to make this easy. It is guesswork. Guesswork based on experience, but still very much guesswork. Every election reveals how often the hired experts turn out to be wrong. So not only would the forces that now control elections be spending much more money. They would be much less certain of getting the results they wanted.

Naturally, they oppose electronic voting.

Chapter 16

Real limits could be put on campaign contributions.

This would be easy to do. All it would take is legislation to that effect.

The open bribery could then be ended if the limits were low enough. The money would not be there. And those who now are able to use the open bribery so much to their advantage would not be able to do so. Because the great differences between the money they can spend and what others can spend would be gone.

Politicians would have less money for their campaigns. But they would all be handicapped equally. They could still campaign. They could give speeches. They could debate. They could do the things politicians used to do to get elected. Those things did not cost very much. What the politicians would have to cut back on would be campaign commercials. Which could be all to the good, since commercials are the greatest source of abuse in campaigns.

Needless to say, the sources that control elections do not want real limits on campaign contributions. At the same time they realize the public sees to some extent the effects large contributions have. So they make occasional gestures toward reducing them. But in fact they leave sufficient loopholes so this does not happen. The contributions just get bigger and bigger.

Chapter 17

So, although there are alternatives to the present system, they will not be put into effect.

It could be worse. The voters do have some control over the system, in contrast to systems that do not have elections. They can get changes made. Because, despite the logic, some of them continue to vote. But the basic system persists. And it gives more power to money than to votes.

X.

Why Self-interest Provides An Understanding Of Human Behavior

Chapter 1

Self-interest provides an understanding of the behavior of human beings.

Behavior in the past. Behavior in the present. Behavior in the future.

Chapter 2

Psychology's attempts to find other explanations have failed.

Chapter 3

What is called self-interest is not self-interest.

Human beings are said to be acting in their self-interest when in fact they are acting in the interest of themselves and those who are close to them.

This is true for adults, who are the ones whose behavior has to be dealt with. What is in their interest is what benefits their families and others who have a special relations to them, not just themselves. So to think of their behavior as selfish is wrong. Though it can look selfish, since what benefits those others often benefits them as well.

In the world before the rise of women families were always represented by men in their dealings outside the family. Women were confined to matters within families. So it was men who made the decisions and took the actions for the families. Which caused them to get the reputation for acting out of self-interest. When they were not doing that except insofar as the families' interest was their interest.

And the non-self-interest element in the situation was greater because of the succession of generations. Men were not motivated solely by the interest of present members of their families and themselves. They were also motivated by concern for the family in the long term. Their family was a continuing institution to which they owed their allegiance and service.

So it is with these qualifications that the term self-interest should be used.

Chapter 4

Self-interest provides an understanding of the behavior of most human beings most of the time. And nothing else does.

Human beings are the only creatures who do not behave in their own self-interest all the time. The term self-interest being qualified so that it includes the interest of whatever other creatures the creatures in question are bound to by instinct.

Human beings are the only creatures who do not behave in their own self-interest all the time because they can feel sympathy. They take this characteristic for granted because they have known it all their lives. (As much of their lives as they can remember.) They do not ask themselves where this characteristic has come from. The answer is simple. It comes from their imagination. But, then, they do not know where their imagination comes from. The answer to that is also simple. Imagination comes from the evolution of thinking. It is impossible to think without imagination. Because thinking requires considering what could happen. Considering that has to be done somewhere. That somewhere is the imagination.

Because human beings have imagination, they can put themselves in the place of others and feel what they imagine others are feeling. They can then want to do something about those feelings of others, which they are feeling themselves.

This is sympathy, and sympathy can make them do for others things that are not in their self-interest.

Since human beings do not always do what is in their self-interest, what each of them will do in any situation cannot be predicted, even though the circumstances of that situation are known well enough so that if they always acted in their self-interest their behavior could be predicted.

But most human beings do do what is in their self-interest most of the time, so the behavior of most of them can be predicted and understood. Again, providing enough circumstances of the situation they are in are known.

Chapter 5

The predominance of self-interest makes understanding human behavior easy.

All a human being has to do is ask what he would do under the same circumstances. Providing he was consulting his self-interest. That is what most other human beings would do. And because that is what most other human beings would do, that is the behavior that will prevail.

Human beings do in fact use this method for explaining the past behavior and predicting the future behavior of one another. But there is much less public admission of this than the real situation warrants, because societies promote various forms of misrepresentation of the matter. They do not want the predominance of self-interest to be admitted.

One consequences of this is that knowledge of the truer situation can be shared only in private speech.

This lack of public admission is exploited by societies as proof that self-interest is not as rampant as it is. That it does not prove that cannt be challenged publicly. Which adds to the illusion.

Chapter 6

Psychology's attempts to find other explanations have failed because motivation cannot be isolated and proved.

Science gets its results because its causes can be isolated and proved. This is done in experiments. Anybody can carry out those experiments and get the same results. That is proof. Psychology cannot do this because motivation is inseparably multiple. That this or that separate motive caused this or that separate result cannot be proved. So psychology cannot explain human behavior, since explanation consists of showing what causes what.

Chapter 7

Psychology attempts to find other explanations have failed because of the limited exercise of free will.

Philosophy has questioned the existence of free will (choice) since it originated. This was ridiculous. Because human beings have intelligence they must have free will. Otherwise intelligence would be useless, since the purpose of intelligence is to make choices.

Philosophy questioned the existence of free will because it came up with a belief in an all-powerful God. If there were an all-powerful God human beings could not choose, since that all-powerful God would be determining everything that happened, including human behavior.

That was one argument against free will. The other argument was materialism. The belief in materialism maintained that if human beings were made up only of matter they could not choose, since matter cannot choose.

The belief in an all-powerful God has been abandoned as science advanced. A belief in an all-powerful God was believable only when other, better explanations were not available. Science has provided those other, better explanations.

The belief in materialism remains, but with a very important change. The belief in materialism had always maintained that life consisted of matter and, therefore, like other matter, could not exercise choice. But science has demonstrated that living matter, in contrast with non-living matter, can exercise choice. By showing that thinking works through electrical impulses. Those impulses are matter and they are the means by which choices are made.

So materialism and free will can be combined.

But the use of free will is limited because of the situations human beings find themselves in. It is advantageous for them to do many things. They have to do many things. They cannot simply behave as they would like to. This leaves psychology little to deal with. It asks: What would human beings do if they could act on their motives? but very often they cannot. That is when self-interest determines their behavior.

Chapter 8

Psychology is left with nothing to give but attention.

Human beings do have psychological problems. And, consequently, do have knowledge about them. Common knowledge. Psychology uses this knowledge. Its original contribution is in vocabulary. It talks and writes about the problems differently than human beings used to do. But psychology does not understand these problems any better. The only real contribution to dealing with them has come from chemistry.

So why do psychologists abound? They are everywhere. A great deal of money is spent on them. They are established. Psychologists abound because they fill a need. A need for experts to deal with problems. The feeling is that something has to be done about them. Psychologists claim that they are able to do something. Undoubtedly, there are some positive results. Whether they are due to the psychologists' intervention or whether they would have happened without it is unknown. There were some positive results when religion dealt with these problems. That did not prove the validity of religion.

What psychology does do of undoubted value is give attention to those suffering psychological problems. That is better than ignoring them. The common knowledge about human behavior attests to that. Those who are suffering like to get attention. It makes them feel better. So psychology has its place.

XI.

Why Agriculture Did Not Suit Human Beings

Chapter 1

Agriculture did not suit human beings.

Chapter 2

But human beings had to adopt agriculture.

Chapter 3

The great advantage human beings have over other creatures is their ability to think.

To think human beings had to be able to detach themselves from reality. They had to be able to see what they were not seeing, hear what they were not hearing, etc. They had to be able to imagine. They had to be able to do this so they could consider imaginary choices. Which is what thinking is.

Nobody knows how human beings acquired the ability to think. Nobody knows when they acquired the ability to think. All that is known is that it was long ago. Weapons and tools are proof.

Human beings used to believe other creatures had the ability to think. It is impossible to just look at other creatures and know whether they can think. Thinking is not visible. Human beings believed other creatures were like them and they were like other creatures. So they believed other creatures could think. They did not realize if they looked at the behavior of other creatures they could tell whether those other creatures could think. Because thinking shows itself in complexity of behavior. The behavior of creatures that can think it much more complex than the the behavior of creatures that cannot think. That is because creatures that can think are choosing some of their behavior with thinking. What they choose with thinking is different from what they would chose if they were letting their bodies do all the choosing for them. As other creatures do.

Chapter 4

Human beings developed thinking in the primitive age because they were not natural predators.

To succeed as predators they had to think a lot. They could not, as most species do, just rely on their instincts. Most predatory species can rely on their instincts because they prey on few creatures. They have their natural victims. The actions needed to prey on these creatures are repetitive. They can be instinctual. Human beings preyed on many creatures. They had to be opportunistic because they were not natural predators. They were not big enough, or strong enough, or fast enough. They started as gatherers, eating meat only occasionally. But they were drawn to predation because meat provides more energy than vegetation. To make up for their deficiencies as predators, human beings had to anticipate the actions of their prey. That was where the thinking came in. Then they could catch and kill the prey. And have food that gave them more energy.

Chapter 5

Predation suited human beings because it kept their two selves occupied.

Other creatures have only one self. Their bodies provide this self with information and tell it what to do. Their bodies tell them to get food, drink water, etc. If their bodies do not tell them to do anything, they do not do anything. They rest, they sleep.

Because they developed thinking, human beings have two selves.

One of those selves is like the single self of other creatures. It does what the body tells it to do.

The other self is consciousness. Consciousness has to have something to occupy it. It can be what the other self is occupied with. Or it can be what imagination and memory occupy it with. Or some combination of the two.

All creatures have memory. That is why they can learn from experience. But they do not have conscious memory. Because they do not have that second self that human beings have. Human beings have conscious memory so they can consider that happened to them in the past when they are making choices. They are not limited to considering only what happened to them. They can imagine as well as remember. They can put together elements in their experience that did not occur together.

Predation suited human beings. It kept their first self active because it required movement and adaptation. It kept their second self active because it required the use of memory and imagination.

Chapter 6

Human beings had to adopt agriculture once they discovered it.

They discovered it by thinking. Agriculture did not just present itself.

Human beings were gatherers. Like many other creatures. They gathered what nature presented with them. They realized—by thinking—they could get more from gathering if they intervened in nature's processes. At first this did not change their style of living. But it did once they got better at it. Then they had to settle down in one place and devote themselves to caring for what they were growing.

Human beings did not do this willingly. They liked hunting. Hunting suited them. But agriculture produced more food. It enabled more of them to live. And those larger numbers could defeat hunters, since hunting produced less food and, accordingly, smaller numbers. Hunting necessarily gave way to agriculture.

Chapter 7

Agriculture did not suit human beings because it was monotonous.

It provided too little for the second self to do.

Agriculture was monotonous because the growing units were small. There had to be many of them. Whatever work was done had to be repeated. Over and over again.

And agriculture was monotonous because vegetation was passive. It could not fight back. It could not run away. It could not choose its behavior like animals.

Because agriculture was monotonous, human beings had to force themselves to do agricultural work. Or be forced to do it. Once agriculture got established, human beings still hunted if they could. The ruling minorities hunted. It was their pastime. They did not work in agriculture. Agriculture was drudgery.

Chapter 8

Agriculture was a disaster for nine-tenths of the human race.

Agriculture caused minority rule. The ruling minorities and their hangers-on made up perhaps one-tenth of the population. The percentage could vary from time to time and place to place. But the variance remained within a narrow range. Far and away the largest number of human beings were those being ruled, not those doing the ruling.

The ruling minorities exploited and ruled majorities. Their objective was to give them just enough of production so they could stay alive and keep working. The ruled majorities had no rights. They could be treated however the minorities chose to treat them.

This was so in all the areas given over to agriculture. The surviving records are proof. The ruling minorities put a favorable interpretation on the situation. But that was because they thought they were the only ones who mattered.

The ruled majorities did not have to put up with only exploitation and subjection. Agriculture caused war along with minority rule. So civilization—as agricultural societies were called—was characterized by the repeated horrors of war.

The disaster for the overwhelming majority of the human race lasted until well into the Industrial Revolution. During which minority rule was replaced by majority rule. And during which poverty was replaced by prosperity. (In some parts of the world. With the probability that the favored parts of the world will increase.)

It can be argued that the disaster paid off because— eventually—it produced the modern world. But that might have seemed like small consolation to those who suffered from agriculture.

Chapter 9

The agriculture age wasted the human capacity for thinking.

When the capacity for thinking developed, it suited the conditions of life for human beings. It served that life.

Men hunted. While they were hunting, both of their selves were occupied. Their normal self was occupied with dealing with the activities of hunting. All the physical activities involved. Their thinking self was occupied with choosing what they would do. Using memory and imagination to think.

At the end of the day men would have some time to themselves. (Usually not much, because they were in competition with other small groups in their area.) With spare time they could think. That is what produced their breakthrough: weapons and tools. They had the time to think them up. And they had the time to make them.

Men followed up on the breakthrough. By the time they went over to agriculture they were a much more advanced species.

Women, meanwhile, had made their contribution. Vegetation was not as stimulating as animal life, but there was great variety and much was added to the human diet and the way of living in general. Very likely, women made the discoveries which led to agriculture.

Once the agricultural age began, men no longer hunted on a regular basis, if at all. The activity thinking had been developed for was no longer available to them. With the exception of the ruling minorities, for whom it was a sport. Their lives did not depend on it. They did not have to think of ways to get more out of it.

A lack of new developments resulted. Wherever agriculture prevailed, generation after generation went on without change. Mediterranean civilization is a good example. The means of production and the ways of production remained practically the same in the whole are of the civilization from its beginning to its end. And the Dark Ages followed. When civilization went backward.

Chapter 10

The modern age revived thinking, but only for a minority of specialists.

Printing caused the modern age. It enabled human beings to preserve more knowledge. It gave thinking something productive to work with.

Knowledge was largely unshared in the agricultural age. There was writing. But it was expensive and limited to the ruling minorities. Who wee interested in governing but not in production. And those engaged in production were not only illiterate and so unable to use writing. They were also unwilling to share what they knew. They wanted to preserve their monopolies in knowledge and so continue to gain from them.

With printing writing became cheap. That made literacy worthwhile for those engaged in production. They could get access to knowledge that was valuable for them. Monopolies of that knowledge were harder to maintain. With printing it took the defection of only one of those acquainted with the knowledge to make it generally available.

But the accumulation and sharing of knowledge did not bring a return of the conditions of the primitive age. When every human being could be an inventor. In the modern age invention required access to resources beyond the means of individuals. This limited it to specialists working for organizations that could afford those resources. The general public could not take part.

Chapter 11

The modern age does not suit human beings as well as the primitive age did.

Most of the work in the modern age is more like agricultural work than hunting.

And there is more idle time.

Work in the advanced countries occupies at most one third of the day. Another third goes to sleeping, Leaving a third for idle time.

Modern human beings cannot use their idle time as did the human beings of the primitive age. The kind of thinking human beings did then has been taken over by specialists. This leaves human beings with a choice between boredom and distraction.

Entertainment has been developed to provide the distraction. It is available 24 hours a day. Unfortunately, human beings are not capable of being entertained for such long periods. The law of diminishing returns applies as much to entertainment as it does to production. A little entertainment can be very much enjoyed. A lot of entertainment becomes boring.

This leaves human being with work that does not engage much of their capabilities and idle time for which there is too little distraction. Neither of the two selves they developed in the primitive age is well served.

XII.

Why Countries That Want To Borrow Abroad Must Have Unfavorable Trade Balances

Chapter 1

Countries that want to borrow money abroad must have unfavorable trade balances.

But this is not well understood. The belief persists that countries can combine favorable trade balances and foreign borrowing.

Chapter 2

Countries like to borrow abroad because then their own populations can spend more.

Their own populations can spend more because they do not have to save very much of their income. Which is what they would have to do if they were going to be the ones loaning money to their government.

Chapter 3

That governments borrow money can be puzzling since they have have the unlimited power of printing money.

It can seem that if governments have an unlimited power of printing money that is what they would do. Then they would have no national debts and would owe no interest.

But if governments print too much money they cause inflation. Inflation ruins economies because—if it is continued long enough—it makes production unprofitable. The value of money falls so fast that what is made from production is too little to pay for continuing that production. So less and less is produced.

This has been proved over and over again by countries that have inflated their currencies too much. They have brought about their own economic collapse.

Chapter 4

Countries that want to borrow abroad must have unfavorable trade balances because otherwise the countries they want to borrow from would not have money to loan them.

Countries that buy as much as they sell abroad have no money to lend to foreign countries. All the money they have which could be used for that goes instead to paying for what they buy abroad. Only if they sell abroad more than they buy do they have money left over they can loan to foreign countries.

In practice countries both buy and invest abroad. The investing includes making loans to foreign countries. No matter how they divide up what they do, they must balance what they buy and invest abroad with what they sell abroad. It is impossible to do otherwise.

Chapter 5

While countries can borrow abroad if they have unfavorable balances of trade, they cannot keep this up indefinitely.

Eventually they will owe so much in interest that their debts will be too great. Their populations will refuse to pay the interest. They will insist that it be reduced.

They can do this because their governments can print whatever amount of money is necessary. Enough can be printed to cause the resultant inflation that will reduce foreign debts to an acceptable level.

Doing this will have bad effects on their own economies. They will accept that rather than put up with what they consider an intolerable level of interest on their national debt.

Chapter 6

Countries used not to be able to print as much money as they wanted to.

Money had been precious metals. It then had a value of its own. It was accepted because of that value. It was not accepted because some government said it had to be.

Banks inspired governments to start using paper money. They had developed their own form of it. Which was pieces of paper that said the banks would pay such and such an amount of real money in exchange for it.

These pieces of paper were easier to deal with than the precious metals themselves. After they were introduced in the later Middle Ages, they were used more and more.

Governments decided they could do what the banks did. They started issuing paper money.

The catch with both banks and governments was that they did not have enough precious metals to exchange for all the paper money they put out. They were always insolvent. The system worked only if not too many of those with paper money tried to exchange it for precious metals. When too many tried, the banks and governments could not pay.

During the Great Depression this system had to be abandoned. The banks could not pay. The governments could not pay. The governments dealt with their problem by saying they would no longer exchange precious metals for their paper money. The governments dealt with the banks' problem by saying they would in future pay what the banks owed. But with paper money, not precious metals.

From then on governments could print as much money as they wanted to.

Chapter 7

Governments gave themselves a big present when they went off the gold standard.

The amount of the big present was the value of however much gold they had.

While countries were on the gold standard, they could not spend their gold. They had to keep it to be able to exchange it for paper money. It was the belief that paper money could be exchanged for gold that gave paper money its value.

What going off the gold standard meant was that governments no longer had to exchange their gold for paper money. So it was theirs to do with whatever they wanted.

The "present" was worth billions of dollars. The amount had to be enough to keep the public thinking their paper money could be exchanged for gold. What was required to do this under normal circumstances could have been as high as 10% of the total paper money circulating in the country.

Little is known about what was done with these landfalls. They were certainly welcomed by the governments that got them. Normal revenues were low because of the Great Depression. Expenses were high because of the public works programs and welfare. The gold went a long way toward making up the difference. There were still deficits, but they were not nearly as great as they would have been otherwise.

Chapter 8

Countries do not admit they are going to pay off their national debts with inflation.

It would be counter-productive to do this. It would make borrowing money difficult, if not impossible.

Countries maintain the fiction that they are going to pay off their national debts. When these debts are being increased, the common complaint is that the cost of maintaining them is going to be borne by future generations. This has popular appeal and does something to slow down the increase in national debts.

But the argument is false. A country will put up with a certain amount of its national income being used to pay interest on its national debt. The amount will vary with the country. But there is bound to be a limit. Once that limit is reached, the voters of the country will demand that something be done to lessen the burden. The only thing that can be done is to inflate the currency. Anything else, like paying off some of the national debt, would increase, not decrease, the burden.

XIII.

Why Consciousness Confused
The Human Species

Chapter 1

Consciousness confused the human species.

Chapter 2

Consciousness confused the human species because it introduced a new kind of existence.

This new kind of existence is the perception of what is not being perceived.

Human beings must have been extremely startled when they first experienced this kind of existence. Like human beings earlier on, most other creatures can perceive only what they are perceiving.

Chapter 3

Consciousness started with memory.

All creatures have memory. Otherwise they could not learn from experience.

But they do not have conscious memory. They cannot perceive again what they have already perceived. The way they learn from experience is different. Their bodies do it. They have no consciousness to take part in the process.

In human beings consciousness started with memory and then went on to imagination. Which combines the elements of memory differently than they occurred. So memory is necessary for imagination. Which explains why it occurred first.

Some other creatures have conscious memory. The proof for this is that they dream. This can be observed when they sleep. Whether they have imagination is uncertain. Behavior does not demonstrate imagination as it does memory. Imagination can only be inferred from the complexity of behavior. That complexity can indicate choices are being made consciously, which requires imagination. But the degree of complexity of behavior that requires imagination is unknown. Some creatures are capable of very complex behavior that could be determined by their bodies alone. So whether only human beings have imagination remains unprovable.

What is certain is that human beings have accomplished the most with imagination. So much so that it puts them in a class by themselves, whether other creatures have some imagination or not.

Chapter 4

Human beings thought the new kind of existence existed without existing.

They did not have the means to know this was false. They went by appearances.

Consciousness could not be known to exist as other forms of existence could be. The heads of human beings could be cut open. No consciousness would be found. It did not seem to have physical existence.

So it was considered to be a new kind of existence. Which it was. And it was considered to be a new kind of existence which did not exist. Which it was not. It did have physical existence. But human beings did not know this at the time.

Chapter 5

Human beings thought the new kind of existence was separate from the body.

They thought this because consciousness is not limited to doing only what the body is doing. If it was limited to that, it could not do what it evolved to do. Which is to make possible the consideration of possibilities. So what seems to be the best one can be chosen for action.

Consciousness can go anywhere. In space or time. It can do anything. Possible or impossible. In contrast with the body. So how could it not be separate from the body?

Chapter 6

Human beings thought the new kind of existence could survive the death of the body.

This was partly because they thought this new kind of existence was separate from the body. And partly because they though it could be perceived after the death of the body.

It seemed logical to them that if this new kind of existence was separate from the body, it would not necessarily die with the body. And they thought they had proof that it did survive the death of the body.

The proof was that they believed they perceived the new kind of existence after the death of the body.

All primitive peoples believe this. It is not a case of some do and some do not.

This belief is no longer generally held. It has been revealed to be without substance.

Chapter 7

The 20th century provided the proof that the new kind of existence could not survive the death of the body.

The poor was that electrical impulses took place in the brain while the new kind of existence was being experienced. The new kind of existence depended on the body. No body, no new kind of existence.

This in itself was enough to prove the new kind of existence could not survive the death of the body. But it was not widely known. What got through to the public was investigations of the cases where the new kind of existence was supposedly perceived after the death of the body. Most of these cases had never been seriously investigated. Somebody's version of the event had been accepted. There was willingness to believe. With the decline of religion the attitude changed. There was an unwillingness to believe rather than a willingness. Serious investigations were made. They showed the alleged events had not happened. By the end of the 20th century the belief such events could happen was discredited. It was no longer part of popular beliefs.

Chapter 8

Human beings believed that all creatures and things were like them and had the new kind of existence.

This was a natural mistake. They could not see that other creatures and things did not have a consciousness like theirs or did not have a consciousness at all. So they went by the evidence they did have: themselves. They had a consciousness, so everything must have a consciousness.

Chapter 9

Human beings had trouble distinguishing between the imaginary and the real.

Consciousness had started for them as memory. Memory brought back the real. They had no trouble distinguishing between what they remembered as real and what was real.

The situation changed with imagination developed. Which it did so they could combine elements in their experience differently than they had occurred. This enabled them to think and make conscious choices. But at the same time it caused the problem of distinguishing between the imaginary and the real.

That was not so easy to do. The imaginary and the real appeared the same in consciousness. They appeared as perceptions. Nothing about their perception in consciousness identified one as real and the other as imaginary. They could be told apart only through asking whether they had occurred in experience.

This was not a necessarily reliable test. Human beings were capable of believing they were perceiving what they were imagining. So they were capable of believing that what they only imagined had actually occurred. And so was real.

Chapter 10

Because human beings could believe the imaginary was real, they believed imaginary powers were controlling their lives.

Different things happened to human beings. Some favorable, some unfavorable. They did not think this was accidental. They thought it was deliberate.

This was logical. Since they believed the rest of the world was like them, they believed what happened was determined the way they determined what they did.

They would have been stumped if they had believed that only what they perceived existed. Then they would have had no explanation. But since they believed the imaginary could exist, they imagined various powers causing what happened to them.

This would not have had such dire consequences if they had not also believed these imaginary powers could be gotten to act one way or the other. And could be gotten to act one way or the other by the same means that worked with them. This caused them to do all sorts of things which were harmful to themselves and others. The harm included inflicting pain and death. And, at the least, wasting prodigious amounts of time.

Chapter 11

Because human beings could believe the imaginary was real, they failed at philosophy.

Philosophy was an attempt to understand the world differently than religion, which claimed that imaginary powers controlled both human beings and nature.

But philosophy did not know that the non-existent could not exist because those who attempted it did not know how consciousness evolved. Which was understandable. They did not know how anything had evolved because they did not know about evolution. So they considered their self-knowledge of consciousness and decided it was a different kind of existence. An existence that did not have to exist. This led them to a long series of false theories which constituted philosophy.

A small minority did maintain that only what existed could exist. But they drew a false conclusion which spoiled what otherwise was a correct philosophy. This conclusion was that human beings could not choose. Since—this philosophy reasoned—their only existence was their physical existence and physical existence cannot choose. That reasoning would eventually be proved false by discoveries about how the brain works. But until then and philosophy created a problem for itself which it could not solve. That problem was to explain the purpose of thinking if human beings could not choose. Because if they could not choose thinking had no purpose.

Chapter 12

Morality has taken over from religion as the greatest cause of confusion for the human species.

The belief in imaginary powers ruling the world has declined dramatically in the last century. But the belief in morality—equally false—has not even been challenged.

And morality has taken on an importance it has never had before. Because with democracy morality has come to determine the outcome of elections.

Before democracy the world was ruled by minorities. Morality was what served their interests. It did not change because their interests did not change.

It would seem logical that with democracy morality would have become what serves the interests of majorities. But this has not happened.

The ruling minorities had the same interests and were united in defending them. Today's majorities have different interests and divide over which interests should be served. Not only do they have different interests, but they often do not know what would serve those interests.

Their recourse is to try to govern by morality.

Unfortunately, morality no longer exists. What it is is what anybody wants it to be. So governing by morality is forcing what some group wants on the remainder of the population. And this group does not have to be, and often is not, the majority of the population. In modern democracy a well-organized minority can triumph over a poorly organized or unorganized majority.

Morality did exist until the decline of religion. The imaginary powers who ruled the world determined what morality was. That gave it an existence independent of individual likes and dislikes. But that existence no longer exists. Like the imaginary powers themselves. So appeals to morality are meaningless.

XIV.

Why "All Men Are Created Equal" Does Not Mean What It Says

Chapter 1

"All men are created equal" did not mean what it said.

It did not confer equal treatment on all men in what would become the United States. Even on all white men.

"All men are created equal" was meant to end the special treatment ruling minorities got. Minorities had ruled the civilized world since civilization began. They conferred special treatment on themselves as part of their domination and exploitation of subject populations.

At the time of the Declaration of Independence the 13 colonies had ruling minorities of their own. But these ruling minorities were subject to another ruling minority in Great Britain. The purpose of the Declaration of Independence was to justify the end of that subjection.

In France the appeal to equality was used against the resident ruling minority. Which a new minority was in the process of displacing.

Chapter 2

"All men are created equal" applied only to the well-off.

Who could vote in the newly-created United States was determined by the states. They had property requirements for voting. Anybody who did not own the required amount of property could not vote.

It is estimated that more than half the white men in the country at the time did not own the required amount of property and so could not vote. Estimates of just how many run as high as 85%. Statistics for this period are far from reliable. But reflection on the nature of the population and the state of the economy confirm that a large percentage of the white male citizens would not have owned enough property to qualify.

So if "all men are created equal" was meant to mean all men would have been able to vote, it turned out to be false.

This gets little attention in the school books used in the American school system. The illusion that all white men could vote is maintained.

Chapter 3

"All men are created equal" is frivolously condemned for not being applied to women, blacks and Indians.

This is one of the countless examples of applying contemporary morality to the past, when conditions were different and contemporary morality does not apply.

Women in the late 18th century were totally dependent on men. That had been the situation from the beginning of civilization. At the time there was no way for them to lessen this dependence, let alone end it. They were confined to the family. They had no place in public life. Their being allowed to vote was not even considered.

Blacks in the late 18th century were slaves. With numerically insignificant exceptions. Treating slaves as equals would have meant ending slavery. Which the country was not in the least disposed to do at the time.

Indians in the late 18th century lived in territories of their own or were remnants in the territory of the United States. They were a hostile force along the borders, since white men were moving west, making wars inevitable. Giving Indians the vote was out of the question.

So condemning "all men are created equal" for not being applied to women, blacks and Indians is not to be taken seriously.

Chapter 4

"All men are created equal" was based on a false philosophy.

All movements have to justify themselves. Otherwise they will not be supported. The justifications can be ridiculous. That does not matter. But they do have to be there.

The false philosophy that the American Revolution was based on was the philosophy of natural rights. Which was developed to counter the philosophy of divine right.

Kings claimed they ruled by divine right. So they should be able to rule autocratically. According to them, God made them kings. Nobody had a right to interfere with their rule.

Kings never did rule autocratically. Given the conditions of the time, it was impossible. But the sharing of power they had to practice was done behind the scenes. They looked as if they were ruling autocratically.

The natural rights philosophy was introduced when the English upper classes decided to institutionalize the power sharing. The philosophy justified the political change by maintaining there were limits on royal power. These limits existed because men had natural rights. Therefore, kings could not do whatever they chose. They had to respect those natural rights.

Where these natural rights came from was never explained. Why they had not been known about previously was never explained. But they were accepted because they suited the occasion.

The American colonists took up natural rights so they could justify their independence movement. Which had become inevitable once they no longer needed Great Britain to protect them after it had driven France out of Canada. The colonists produced no substantial new thinking on the philosophy, but simply accepted it as it had been originally formulted.

Chapter 5

Nature did not intend all men to be created equal.

What happened in nature to living creatures was determined by evolution.

Evolution depends upon creatures being different, not alike. That they are born different makes them unequal. Some are better able to cope with their environment than others. Those are the ones that survive and reproduce.

Chapter 6

Human beings came as close to equality as they ever got when they lived together in small groups.

This happened during the period when they developed enough to be human beings and before they discovered agriculture.

The conditions of this life made it democratic. The members of the group lived together in small numbers. The greatest force within the group was a majority. No single man and no minority could effectively oppose the greater numbers.

The conditions of this life were egalitarian. Like other forms of life, it was on a subsistence level. All adults had to be kept alive so the group would have sufficient numbers to protect itself against neighboring groups. All children had to be kept alive so when older members died there would be replacements.

Chapter 7

Agriculture ended equality for human beings.

Agriculture caused ruling minorities. The organized force of these minorities dominated the disorganized majorities.

Agriculture ended subsistence living. More was produced than was needed to keep human beings alive. The ruling minorities appropriated this for themselves. They found other uses for it than subsistence.

Without political or economic equality, equality for human beings was impossible.

Chapter 8

"All men are created equal" was confined to voting and the legal system.

But even there it did not mean what it said.

Voting is only part of the political system. Control of that system is divided between voting and other factors. Money being the most important of those other factors. Even when all adults came to vote, as happened, voters do not have political equality.

The legal system is like the political system. It can seem to confer equality when it does not. It can say all men are equal under the law, but that is only one factor so long as other factors affect the application of the law. As they do. Again, money being the most important of those other factors.

That the system does not provide political or legal equality is not to say that it imposes as much inequality as previous systems. It does not. It is to say that it does not provide equality, so that "all men are created equal" is not true. As it was never meant to be. It was meant to deceive, and it did that.

XV.

Why The Cause Of The Civil War Was Obvious And Simple

Chapter 1

The cause of the Civil War was obvious and simple. But it was not publicly admitted at the time. And it is not publicly recognized today.

Chapter 2

The cause of the Civil War was the value of the slaves. It was too great.

The South was not going to give away its slaves. The North was not going to pay for them. This made the Civil War inevitable.

Chapter 3

There were approximately five million blacks in the United States at the time of the Civil War. The great majority of them were slaves. It they were valued at an average of $1,000 each, setting them free would have cost hundreds of billions of dollars. Even if the valuation were much less, the total still would have run into the billions.

One billion dollars at the time was an unthinkable amount of money. Governments did not deal in billions of dollars then. They did not even come close. The North might have been willing to free the slaves for some much lower amount of money. Other countries did where many fewer slaves were involved. But the magnitude of the cost in the United States was just too much.

Chapter 4

Great Britain bought out its slaveowners in the 1830s.

The number of slaves in the British possessions as much lower than the number of slaves in the United States. And the whole of Great Britain bore the cost. Whereas in the United States the number was much higher and only half the country—the North—would have borne the cost.

Once the slaveowners in the British Caribbean were paid off, their plantations continued to be run much as before. The world still wanted plantation products. The blacks still needed work. The ex-slaveowners had much the same income as before and much the same capital. The difference was that the capital no longer consisted of slaves.

Chapter 5

Because of the impossibility of a British-like settlement, the South tried to maintain political equality with the North.

With political equality the South could prevent the expropriation of its slaves and otherwise hold its own against the North.

To maintain political equality the South had to acquire new states. The problem was that most of the remaining land available was not suited to slavery.

A peculiarity of the U.S. political system made it possible for the South to maintain political equality despite its much smaller population. The U.S. Constitution had introduced a federal system because the new country was a combination of separate areas. Under the system each of the previously separate areas had equal representation in the upper house. And the upper house was equal to the lower house, which represented population.

This was clearly undemocratic, but the realities of the situation made it necessary.

The South had enough states to give it equal power with the North for 70 years. What brought on the Civil War was that because of geography the new states sided more and more with the North. And the area remaining to be incorporated into the country was like those new states, not like the states of the South.

This caused the South to start the Civil War, since it believed its position would only get worse with time. Because it could not maintain political equality, it wanted independence.

Chapter 6

The North wanted to weaken and intimidate the South so the South would never rebel again. That the war and the freeing of the slaves would do this was shown by the subsequent history of the United States. The South was permanently subdued.

The North could not free the slaves at the beginning of the war because some slaves states were fighting on its side. Freeing the slaves was a political impossibility. But once the war was won, these states were helpless. They had to accept the freeing of the slaves just as did the states that had fought with the South. The North no longer had anything to fear from them.

Chapter 7

The North had never thought out how it would deal with the South after the Civil War.

This is true of the politicians as well as the general public. When the end of the war came, a small minority of abolitionists dominated the government of the North. They gave ex-slaves the vote. They helped ex-slaves get into politics.

But they did not confiscate the property of the ex-slaveholders. It was only a matter of time before those men, with property as their base, would take over the government of the South again.

Initially, the North occupied the South. There was public support for this because of the hatred the war had caused. But the hatred abated with time. And the general public was confronted with the reality in the South.

There had never been widespread popular support in the North for abolition. Racial prejudice was general. So when the occupation of the South turned out to be costly and difficult, the North abandoned it. After little more than 10 years.

De facto slavery took the place of the old slavery. And lasted well into the 20th century.

Chapter 8

Because of the early end of the slave trade, the South was able to substitute sharecropping for slavery.

The slave trade to the United States had been ended in 1808. By the time of the Civil War slaves in the country had been domesticated. They were ready for sharecropping.

This did not happen in Central or South America or in the Caribbean. The difference was that slaves in the United States had been born and raised there. Elsewhere in the Americas large numbers were still being imported from Africa. The end of the slave trade applied only to the United States. It was the only slave country that bred all its own slaves.

Slaves imported from Africa would not have been able to deal with sharecropping. They would not have known the language. On their own they would not have known what to do. The methods of cultivating the crops were not the same. The draft animals were not the same. These slaves had to be used on plantations, where their work was supervised and driven.

Sharecropping was forced on the South by the freeing of the slaves. It turned out to be more productive than the plantations.

With sharecropping the ex-slaves did not have to be supervised. They were not going to run away from their livelihood. They did not have to be driven. They had an incentive to work and to work well, since they shared the crops they produced. This meant lower costs and higher productivity for the owners.

And for the owners additional profits came from the general stores they ran. They no longer had to provide food, clothes and other supplies to the ex-slaves. They could sell these and make more money doing that.

Defeat in the Civil War did not end fortunes in the South. It just changed how they were made.

Chapter 9

The South had to govern by illegal means.

The South offended public opinion in the North—and elsewhere—because it governed by illegal means. Lynchings were notorious. Other lesser forms of mistreatment of the blacks occurred regularly. The adverse public opinion would have been greater had the true conditions in the South been known. They were not because the South conspired to keep them from being reported in the North. And the North joined the conspiracy because it did not want to be reminded of the situation in the South.

The South had to violate federal law because the Civil War gave the blacks rights incompatible with the southern system. By the constitutional amendments the North passed the blacks would have been able to vote and otherwise get equal treatment under the law. Attempts were made to enforce these amendments, but they ended after a few years.

The South used a system of popular justice to subject the blacks. Every white man could give orders to the blacks and punish them if he saw fit. He had arbitrary police authority which he could use at any time.

This was meant to terrorize the blacks so they would submit and not seek legal recourse. Which would have been useless anyhow, since only white southerners served on the courts in the South.

The popular justice system could have been harder on the blacks much of the time than slavery itself. It was usually the rougher elements in the white population who took it upon themselves to administer justice to the blacks. They could be arbitrary, capricious and cruel. The blacks had no value for them. And they were backed by the community. That was essential for the system to work. In contrast, slaveowners had been dealing with their own property. Injured slaves were not going to be able to work. Dead slaves were worthless. Owners could get carried away, but generally they chose to be practical. They punished their slaves, but with calculation and therefore moderation.

Chapter 10

De facto slavery ended because of the migration of blacks to the North.

For de facto slavery to end in the South the federal government had to intervene. The North had given up on its first intervention in 1876. Left as it was, the North would not have intervened again.

What caused the change was the increased number of

blacks in the North. There was work for them there. The big surges came during the two world wars.

The difference between the North and the South was that the North obeyed federal laws. After the Civil War those provided that the blacks could vote and otherwise take part in politics. So as more blacks moved to the North, the black vote increased. And increased and increased. Eventually, the blacks were able to force the politicians they were voting for to get the North to intervene again in the South. That was what ended de facto slavery.

XVI.

Why Private Talk Is Secret

Chapter 1

The world of private talk is secret. But much of what goes on is knowable only through private talk.

Chapter 2

The only way of knowing what goes on in the world of private talk is through speculation.

But speculation cannot be proved. (Except in rare cases.) So speculation can always be denied and so made to seem false.

Chapter 3

Cynicism is the only alternative to access to private talk.

Cynicism is condemned in public talk. It is condemned because it reveals truths that public talk does not want revealed.

Cynicism assumes that individual human beings usually act in their own interest. With their own interest including the interest of those they are attached to. It admits that they do not always act like this. Which is based on common observation. When it comes to organizations of human beings, cynicism assumes that they always act in their interest. This is likewise based on common observation.

With these assumptions cynicism can speculate about human behavior with a high degree of accuracy.

Chapter 4

Since cynicism cannot be expressed in public talk, its extent is unknown.

Human beings do become more cynical as they grow older. As children they are given a false view of life. This is necessary. They could not be trained otherwise. When they get older, they gradually discover the deception. They see it. They learn bout it through the private talk they have access to.

But they do not always acknowledge beliefs that are condemned. They find out there are negative consequences for doing this. So judgments about their degree of cynicism can be incorrect.

Chapter 5

Democracy gave the public an interest in private talk it had never had before.

Until the advent of democracy the developed world had been ruled by minorities. What the public thought had nothing to do with government. These minorities conducted their business through private talk. They felt no obligations to inform the public about what they were doing.

With democracy the public acquired an interest in government. But it did not acquire access to the private talk by which government was conducted. So it had nothing to fall back on but cynicism. Which was condemned. And therefore did not appear in public talk. The result was ignorance about what government was doing and how it was being done. Yet with democracy the public was supposed to be informed about government.

Chapter 6

Democracy forced the use of public talk about government.

With democracy representatives of the public are elected to run the government. To reach this public they have to use public talk.

They cannot tell the truth in public talk, since the truth would be unacceptable. The truth has to be reserved for private talk. Since the public is not told the truth, it is ignorant. And its ignorance is exploited.

That is half the political formula. The other half is the exploitation of emotionalism.

Human beings had emotions before they had thinking. Emotions tell them how to feel and feeling tells them how to act. But thinking is more practical and effective. That is why it developed.

For thinking to be used a situation has to be known. Since the public does not know the situations in politics, it cannot use thinking. It has to fall back on emotions.

Chapter 7

The ignorance and emotionalism of the public came to matter much more when governments became interventionist.

This started on a large scale with the Great Depression. Before that governments let the system work pretty much by itself.

Governments intervened because the system did not seem to be recovering. Labor was helped out. Business was helped out. The intervention was meant to be temporary. But it turned out to be permanent.

The intervention gave the public much more power over how things were divided up. So their ignorance and emotionalism had more effect. Much of what the system used to determine was now determined by the public— because of democracy.

Chapter 8

Despite the effects of private talk on democracy, there has been no movement to put an end to it in government.

When putting an end to it has become feasible.

The ruling minorities of the agricultural age took private talk in government for granted. They had no interest in informing the majorities about what they were doing. And, besides, there was no means of preventing private talk.

When democracy started replacing minority rule, the problem of means remained. Ending private talk was impossible.

The situation did not change until the development of the new technology. Now private talk can be prevented. What governments are actually doing could be known. Public talk could no longer rely for its acceptance on ignorance.

There was not been a movement to promote the end of private talk in government because it has always existed. Which causes it to be considered a right. But a little thought shows that the harm done to democracy by private talk in government is so great that it should be ended. Real democracy cannot exist with private talk in government. After all, why should governments be able to operate secretly? Who conferred that right on them?

XVII.

Why The Universe Did Not Exist Before Life

Chapter 1

The universe did not exist before life.

Chapter 2

For something to exist it has to be capable of being perceived.

Only life can perceive. Without life nothing was capable of being perceived.

Chapter 3

Perception can be real perception or it can be imagined perception.

Real perception is the kind of perception all forms of life are capable of.

There are two kinds of imagined perception.

One kind of imagined perception is perception of what can only be imagined. What can only be imagined does not exist.

The other kind of perception is perception of what could be perceived if circumstances made that possible. What could be perceived like this does exist.

The universe exists because of the second kind of imagined perception. It cannot actually be perceived but it could be if circumstances made that possible.

Circumstances did not make that possible until the existence of advanced human beings. Because those human beings were capable of the second kind of imagined perception.

Chapter 4

Human beings think the universe existed before life because they do not realize existence depends on perception.

Existence does not depend only on perception. It also depends on something being there to be perceived.

Before life existence depended on an impossible condition. Which was that perception was possible. What depends on an impossible condition is impossible.

Human beings do not realize existence depends on perception because they have perception and so they take it for granted. This causes them to think that whatever is capable of being perceived does exist. Which is true so long as there is perception. But which is not true if there is no perception. And there was no perception throughout most of the existence (?) of the universe. There were lots of things there that could have been perceived if there had been perception. But there was not.

Chapter 5

Real perception did not establish the existence of the universe.

Real perception began with the beginning of life. All forms of life perceive. They are aware of other things through their senses. They have to be so they can react.

But only one form of life—the human species—can imagine. As far as we know for sure. And at most only a few forms. And then not enough to establish the existence of the universe.

Real perception establishes the existence of whatever is perceived. But that is all. It does not establish the existence of anything beyond that.

Chapter 6

Imagined perception established the existence of the universe.

Real perception is very limited. It can take in only an infinitesimal part of the universe.

Imagined perception is not limited. It can imagine what is only imaginary. And it can imagine what exists but cannot be perceived by real perception.

That is what it does with the universe.

But how much of the universe is imagined depends upon how much knowledge of the universe there is. Until a few centuries ago human beings—practically speaking—knew only as much of the universe as they could perceive. Discoveries since then have enabled them to imagine much more. But their knowledge is still limited. How limited they do not know. The know that they would have to have knowledge of the part of the universe they do not have knowledge of.

XVIII.

Why The Intervention Of The United States In World War I Caused World War II

Chapter 1

The intervention of the United States in World War I caused the unconditional surrender of Germany. And the unconditional surrender of Germany caused World War II.

World War I was in a stalemate. The countries involved had been fighting three years. Neither side had been able to break through the lines formed by the trenches. Millions of men had been killed. Various new weapons had been tried. None had brought about victory.

The war would not have gone on much longer. Both sides were exhausted. There would have been a negotiated peace.

The intervention of the United States changed the situation. It was not only that one side then had new men and new resources. But that that would have been only the beginning if the war had continued. The United States had a large population. It had a thriving economy. What it put into the war would have kept increasing.

With this overwhelming advantage, the Allies and the United States insisted on unconditional surrender. The enemy soon accepted those terms. There was no alternative but an invasion and utter defeat.

Chapter 2

The unconditional surrender of Germany caused the victorious powers to impose impossible peace terms.

This was largely on the insistence of France.

France and Germany were traditional enemies. France had been defeated in the previous war and had been forced to give up border territory. The temptation to get back at Germany was irresistible. Germany was to be made to pay for the damage done to France during the war. The amount was so great that it could only wreck the German economy. Which it did.

At the same time, Germany had been turned into a democracy. This was on the insistence of the United States, whose president believed that other countries should have the same form of government as his own.

Eventually, the combination of impossible peace terms and democracy enabled an extremist political group to take power in Germany. The purpose of this group was to undo the results of World War I. Which it tried to do in World War II.

Had the United States not intervened in World War I and had the war ended in a negotiated peace, the victorious powers would not have been able to impose such peace terms. They would have had to be more moderate and the reaction in Germany would not have been so extreme. The World War II took place could have been avoided.

Chapter 3

The United States had no national interests that required its entry into World War I.

The intervention took place because the form of government in the United States enables a president to start a war.

Germany and its allies were not threatening any U.S. possessions. The trade of the United States with Europe and its colonies would not have been hurt by a negotiated peace. Europe itself would have remained much the same.

It was President Wilson who decided on the intervention. He proclaimed that World War I was a war to end all wars. Which was ridiculous. He said that permanent peace could be maintained by a League of Nations. When he knew that the league would be powerless so long as the nations making it up retained their sovereignty. Which they had every intention of doing.

It was good propaganda. What Wilson really thought can never be known.

Wilson had an issue that was easy to manipulate: sending supplies to the two sides in World War I.

The British had a surface fleet that could blockade Germany. So Germany could not get supplies from the United States.

The Germans had an underwater fleet. This could blockade England and France. But to do that it had to sink ships, while the British surface fleet had only to turn them back.

The American public did not like ships being sunk. Crews and passengers were drowned. It particularly did not like Americans being drowned. Wilson had only to get Germany to sink ships with Americans aboard. Which he did. That provided him with enough support for a U.S. entry into the war. It may not have been majority support but it was enough.

The U.S. Constitutions stipulates that only the Congress can declare war. Which would seem to settle the matter. But at the same time it makes the president commander-in-chief of the armed forces. As such he can get his country into a position where it will have to go to war.

XIX.

Why The Combination Of Globalization And The Welfare State Threatens Permanent Unemployment

Chapter 1

The combination of globalization and the welfare state threatens permanent unemployment for millions of workers in advanced countries.

With globalization jobs requiring the least qualifications go to developing countries because the pay is lower there. That costs workers in advanced countries their jobs.

The way to deal with this problem would seem to be to train workers in advanced countries for jobs that require higher qualifications. Then they would not only find new employment but they would be better paid.

But that has not happened. The workers in the advanced countries remain unemployed. They can because they are supported by the welfare state.

As globalization increases, the situation will get worse.

Chapter 2

The question is: can the workers in advanced countries be trained for jobs that require higher qualifications?

Chapter 3

Through most of history jobs have not been very demanding. Normal human beings could do them.

Until the 19th century most jobs were in agriculture. Children learned how to do them as they were growing up. They were well within human capacity.

The first jobs the Industrial Revolution created were the same. They did not require special qualifications.

A change took place after World War II. More and more jobs began to require special qualifications. Not everybody could do them. Because of that they required extra training.

These are the jobs that unemployed workers would have to be qualified for.

Chapter 4

Jobs that require extra training can be jobs that not everybody can do.

Some of them can be jobs that everybody can do if trained long enough. But not all of them. And fewer proportionately as production gets more sophisticated.

Human beings have different levels of capacity. This has been demonstrated as education has become more general. Some students do better than others. The grading system reflects this.

It is not only different levels of capacity that cause students to perform differently. It is different levels of application. There are two variables.

Chapter 5

How many unemployed will result because not everybody can do or will do the necessary training is not knowable.

But indications are the number will be high.

Workers who have lost their jobs to cheap labor overseas have not shown much adaptability. They are older. They do not learn as fast. They have families and homes. It is hard for them to start over again. Even if the welfare state pays for them to do that.

And the young have not responded very well to the new situation. Those who have less capacity get discouraged in school and give up. And the young in general, because of their inexperience, do not realize what will be required of them in life. They tend to think the future will take care of itself. They do not apply themselves sufficiently.

Chapter 6

Limiting imports would seem to be the solution to the unemployment problem.

But it is not that easy.

The thinking behind the limit-imports argument is simple. Higher prices could be charged at home because there would be less foreign competition. Then workers could be paid higher wages and factories would not have to be closed.

The argument commonly used against this argument is true but ineffective. It is that worldwide production would be at its greatest if competition were allowed to prevail. The cost of everything would be reduced to its lowest possible level. Production would be maximized. There would be more of everything.

This is so. But the argument is ineffective because it is intellectual. It has to be thought out. It does not demonstrate itself in daily life as the argument for limiting imports does.

The argument that makes much of business favor allowing imports is also intellectual. But it is effective because the thinking behind it is simple.

This thinking is that for a country to sell more abroad it has to buy more abroad. The public does not pay attention to this argument because it is not involved in selling exports. The businesses that are know from daily experience that foreign countries cannot buy from them unless the businesses have the money to do it. And they get that money by selling in their country. That's why these businesses are against limiting imports. They know it would limit their sales.

Chapter 7

Countries would have to buy abroad exactly as much as they sell abroad if it were not for two alternatives.

They can sell abroad more than they buy abroad if they do not try to exchange all the foreign currency they earn for their own currency. They can avoid doing this by investing that foreign currency abroad. The other alternative is to give it away abroad.

Two kinds of investment are available to them abroad. One is buying. The other is loaning.

There are disadvantages to both.

Buying investments abroad contributes to the economy of the foreign country, not to the economy of their own country. Loaning abroad aggravates the problem of exchanging the foreign currency for their own. Because the loans pay interest to them. So as time goes by they have more and more foreign currency to exchange.

Despite the disadvantages, countries often choose to invest abroad because it spares their own economies from some of the competition they would otherwise have to deal with. It does this because it reduces imports. And investing abroad is a form of saving. This is one way to get around the difficulty of saving in welfare states, where governments are always under pressure to spend.

Giving away part of foreign exchange is not as quixotic as it may seem. Developed countries do this with developing countries so those countries' economies will improve and, hopefully, will then buy more from the donor countries. There are also political considerations. The developed countries are more likely to get what they want out of the developing countries. Gifts bring results.

Chapter 8

What seems to be the only solution to the problem may turn out to be not the solution.

Higher pay in the developing countries seems to be the only solution to the problem. This will happen. The present developed countries have no permanent monopoly on what makes them developed—and so more prosperous than the other countries of the world. Many of those other countries are already well on their way to catching up. Eventually all, or almost all, will. The pay for their workers will be the same as the pay in the countries where it was once so much higher. Workers in any one country will no longer be in danger of losing their jobs to cheaper workers elsewhere.

But the problem that started after World War II will steadily become a bigger problem. That is that jobs will require higher qualifications. While more and more of the jobs that do not will be mechanized or otherwise cease to exist. There just may not be enough jobs that workers can quality for, either because of lack of capacity or lack of application. The less qualified will be permanently unemployable. Then the qualified will have to support the unqualified indefinitely.

XX.

Why Has Economics Failed
To Explain What Causes
Recoveries—And What Does

Chapter 1

Economics has failed to explain what causes recoveries. So what does cause them?

Chapter 2

Economics has failed to explain what causes business cycles in general. So what does cause them?

Chapter 3

The Keynesian proposals for dealing with recessions and depressions have become popular again.

So have the opposite proposals.

This has happened because of the economic collapse of 2008. Ways are being looked for to bring back prosperity.

Keynes thought only demand mattered. So he proposed that governments increase demand after a collapse. The increase in demand had to be done by government deficit spending. Since if it was done by spending from regular tax revenue, it would just be taking money from some to give to others. Over-all demand would not be increases.

Those whose proposals are the opposite of Keynes think it is supply that matters. So they propose that governments increase supply after a collapse. The increase in supply after a collapse achieved by lowering taxes. Then, supposedly, more will be invested in production and so supply will increase. And the increase in supply will cause an equal increase in demand.

Chapter 4

Both the Keynesian proposals and the opposite proposals are based on bad reasoning.

Chapter 5

The Keynesian proposals are based on the reasoning that an increase in demand from government deficit spending will cause a much greater increase in national production.

So a government—supposedly—can end a slump with relatively little deficit spending. And that could easily be made up through taxation during the ensuing prosperity.

This reasoning is based on a very strange theory about money. That is that if it is spent over and over again, its effect on demand will be multiplied. So a relatively small amount of stimulus will—supposedly—cause a large increase in the amount of demand. That is Keynes' multiplier effect.

The theory is very strange because it shows ignorance by Keynes of how money works.

Additional money does increase demand. The question is: by how much? If the money a government gives out as stimulus could be spent only once, it would increase demand only once. Demand would fall back to whatever it was before. But money is not spent only once. Somebody spends it. Somebody else gets it. That somebody else spends it. And then another somebody else gets it and spent it. And so on.

So does money increase demand by how many times it is spent? The answer is yes. But the answer does not mean what it seems to mean.

If a government puts a certain amount of new money into its economy, that certain amount of new money will increase demand by its own amount. Providing the number of times money is spent remains the same.

Only if the number of times money is spent in a given period increases will the new money increase demand by more than its own amount. Such increases do not normally happen. So Keynes' multiplier effect normally will not happen. It is an illusion. Production and income will not increase much more than the amount of new money.

Chapter 6

Governments can increase the number of times money is spent in a given period. But doing that can be ruinous.

They can do this by increasing the amount of new money that is created. Increasing the amount of new money causes inflation. How much inflation depends on how much new money is created.

Some inflation is considered a good thing. Governments like it because it means they can spent more than they take in. Businesses like it because it makes their sales and profits increase. The public likes it because it causes more jobs and higher pay.

The amount of inflation that does this has to be enough to get those effects but not so much as to cause runaway inflation. Runaway inflation happens when prices start going up so much that those with money spent it faster than they normally would. They do this because if they spend it only as fast as they normally would, they get less for their money.

With normal inflation—the kind that governments, business and the public like—they get less for their money if they spend it at the normal rate. But how much less it not enough to really matter to them. So they do not speed up how fast they spent their money.

Runaway inflation is called that because the higher the rate of inflation becomes, the faster money is spent.

Runaway inflation ruins economies. Less and less is produced. This happens because what is received for production is not enough to keep production continuing at the same rate. And the effect is cumulative. Productions gets lower and lower.

This happens although whoever is going the producing is making money, because the price productions brings in when it is finished is higher than what it cost. Because prices have been going up while the production took place. But what the production bring in is not enough to produce that much again. To do that would cost more than what it brought in. Given the rapidly rising prices for things in general. So whoever is doing the producing will not be able to produce as much the next time around. And this is what will happen each time around. Less and less is produced over-all. The process can be ended only by starting all over again with a new currency.

Because runaway inflation ruins economies, governments are reluctant to increase the number of times money is spent in a given period. Which means that whatever stimulus they provide during a slump cannot have the multiplier effect described by Keynes.

Chapter 7

Because the Keynes' multiplier does not work, a government cannot provide enough stimulus to cause a recovery.

For a stimulus to cause a recovery, it would have to be a large part of the income lost in a collapse. This would be more than any stimulus ever provided. And sure to be politically unacceptable.

Whatever stimulus a government does provide will lessen the extent of the collapse by whatever amount it is. So it can be said to do some good. But it will not in itself bring about a recovery.

Chapter 8

The proposals of Keynes' opponents are based on the reasoning that lowering taxes will increase investment and so bring about a recovery.

That lowering taxes will bring about a recovery is true. But the question is by how much. There is no guarantee that the amount will be enough to bring about a recovery. There is no guarantee that the amount will be enough to offset how much government revenue will be lost through the lowering of taxes.

Lowering taxes does increase the amount available for investment. But that does not mean it automatically increases investment itself.

Those with income large enough so that they have money left over for investment do not have to invest. They have enough to live on as they are. Investment is an option for them, not a necessity.

And the larger the income the less incentive for investment that involves much risk and so is more productive. Given the situation, they can see themselves as better off with a smaller additional income from a less risky investment than a possibly larger additional income from a more risky investment. So exempting the most wealthy from tax increases does not have the same effect as exempting the less wealthy. Who, given their situation, are ready to take more risk.

So lowering taxes for the wealthiest does not have a predictable effect. It can have much more effect because they have much more they could invest. But it can have much less effect because they have less incentive to do the kind of investment that would contribute the most to recovery.

Chapter 9

Hereditary aristocracies are getting bigger, wealthier and more powerful in democracies.

In the 18th, 19th and 20th centuries democracies have replaced aristocracies as the form of government. Positions in government are elected, not inherited. But this has not meant the disappearance of aristocracies. Wealth is still inherited, as it was when aristocracies ruled. It is wealth that still gives aristocracies their special position. It is wealth that makes them what they are.

Aristocracies have gotten bigger because there is so much more wealth. When aristocracies ruled, wealth came primarily from land. There was only so much land. So there were only so many aristocrats. There was not enough wealth from land to support more. In the modern world wealth comes from production of all kinds. And the total keeps increasing. It is not fixed as it was when aristocracies ruled. The tremendous increase in wealth has enabled many more families to get rich. Much, much richer than the old aristocratic families used to be.

Wealth is power under all forms of government. The outcome of elections in democracies depends upon money as well as votes. It makes possible getting the things done that have to be done. Including the presentation of issues to the public. Voters determine the outcome of elections. But money has much to do with which outcome they choose. That is what gives the hereditary aristocracies their power. They can and do invest heavily in elections. And what follows elections, when government decisions are being made.

Hereditary aristocracies are dependent on government decisions. They could be wiped out if the inheritances were highly taxed. This has not happened. Which is shown by their continued existence and increase in numbers.

Some governments at some times have taxed incomes and

inheritances at higher rates than usual. And the hereditary aristocracies have maintained they were being destroyed. But this was not so. Because tax laws can be circumvented. The hereditary aristocracies have the wealth to employ the experts who can do the circumventing. And they have the wealth to get the laws that are hostile to them changed. They have survived all the attempts to tax them out of existence. They have gotten more numerous, not less numerous. They have gotten wealthier, not poorer. And they have gotten more powerful, now less powerful.

Chapter 10

Since Keynes' proposals and the proposals of his opponents will not work, what will work?

Chapter 11

To understand what will bring about a recovery, it is necessary to understand what causes business cycles in general.

Banks are the cause of business cycles. They are because they create a kind of money different from regular money. They can not only create this kind of money. They can make it disappear. And it can disappear when they do not want it to. This means the amount of their kind of money varies, and varies in such large quantities that it causes capitalist economies to go through business cycles. When there is much of this money demand is high. Prosperity. When there is little of this money demand is low. Recession or depression.

Chapter 12

How banks caused business cycles:

They started out by keeping gold for others. Who thought it was safer with them. They decided they could loan some of it out, making money by charging interest. They did not loan out the gold itself, but pieces of paper which could be exchanged for gold. They were easier to deal with than gold itself.

Then banks made their big discovery. They found they could loan out more in pieces of paper than they actually had in gold. That was because the people the gold belonged to did not often ask to have it back. They preferred to leave it with the banks.

This was what gave the banks the power to create money. The pieces of paper they gave out in loans were treated as money. They could be used to buy things.

(This happened before governments started putting out pieces of paper as money. They were still using metals.)

Because of their discovery, banks could increase or decrease the money supply. They could make more loans or fewer loans.

Banks did not reveal their discovery. Because they knew if the customers who left gold with them realized they could not pay it all back, they would ask to have it back, hoping they would be among the first to do this and so get some of the gold the banks actually had.

Banks were bound to fail at intervals. They made their money charging interest. The more pieces of paper they put out, the more interest they earned. So they kept putting out more pieces of paper.

This caused prosperity. But prosperity could not last.

Prosperity caused rising prices because of the greater amount of pieces of paper banks were putting out. The rising prices started speculation. in whatever parts of the economy that were involved, prices went up because they had been going up and were expected to continue going up. This could last only so long. Prices could not go up forever. There was a collapse. Prices started falling, and the more they fell the more they kept falling.

Those who put gold in banks became afraid the banks could not pay it back. Because that was what had happened in the past. They tried to get their gold back. But banks did not have enough gold to pay back large numbers. They went bankrupt. And the more of them that went bankrupt, the worse the situation became.

Eventually, the whole business cycle sequence repeated itself. The banks that were left started loaning out their kind of money again. That they did improved business. Because business was improving, more was borrowed. Which further improved business. Until prosperity returned. Only to be followed by another collapse.

Chapter 13

Governments started using paper money with nothing behind it during the Great Depression.

They could do this because they could force acceptance of the money.

Before the Great Depression governments had to be ready to exchange their paper money for gold or silver. Since they had only limited amounts of these precious metals, they could create only limited amounts of paper money.

Actually, governments could never exchange all of their paper money for precious metals. They did not have enough. But they maintained the pretext that they could. It was when this pretext would have been put to the test during the Great Depression that governments decided they would no longer try to keep it up and forced acceptance of paper money with nothing behind it. But while the pretence lasted it did limit the amount of paper money they could create. So once they gave it up they were in a new situation.

(Governments had used paper money with nothing behind it before the Great Depression. They did this during wars when they could not meet their greatly increased expenses with regular money. The result was inflation, so when the wars ended they thought they had to go back to precious metals. They discovered during the Great Depression that this was not true, so they kept paper money with nothing behind it. This allowed them much more freedom in spending than the old system did. But they did have to restrain themselves to some extent because of the danger of runaway inflation.)

Chapter 14

Given the modern situation with paper money, governments could save all the banks during an economic collapse.

This would prevent the sudden big reduction in the money supply that characterizes a collapse. And it would enable banks to continue making loans as before. So the collapse would be stopped before it really got started.

Until now governments have saved only some of the banks. Usually the biggest. That is why there have been recessions and depressions.

Governments have taken to saving on the biggest banks because if they failed the whole system would fail with them. The failure of the biggest banks would cause so much money to disappear that the loans the other banks had made would go bad. There would not be enough money to pay them back. So the other banks would fail.

Saving the biggest banks keeps the worst from happening. But other banks can still fail, given there is less money. And they do.

Saving all the banks would require great sums of money. It would be equivalent to providing enough stimulus to make up for all the production lost in a collapse. The public, which does not understand banking, would never accept it. And would be less inclined to if they did understand banking, because then they would know the banks were to blame for the collapse.

It is not only that large numbers of banks fail during a collapse that recovery starts so slowly and takes so long. It is because so many banks that survive cannot loan money on the scale they did before. Given all their loans that have gone bad, their worth is very much diminished. There has to be some ratio between that worth and how much they loan out. So they can loan out much less. Credit is supposedly "frozen". It is not. The banks made fewer loans because they do not have the means to make more, not because they do not want to.

Chapter 15

Governments could most successfully promote recovery by making investments pay better.

This can be done by giving subsidies to business and making tax changes that benefit business.

Recovery can take place only if production increases. Business determines production. Businesses will increase production if they make more money by doing that. Governments can help them make more money by reducing their costs through subsidies and tax changes.

Investment that increases production does so by much more than the amount contributed to it by government through subsidies and tax changes. This is why it is so superior to government stimulus. So such investment has a multiplier effect that government stimulus lacks. That is why it promote recovery much more than government stimulus. That is why it is the most successful way to promote recovery.

Chapter 16

Business cycles will be allowed to continue because they increase production.

Production has vastly increased since business cycles began. That is because bank money makes possible much more investment than only regular money would.

With only regular money investment is limited to what is left over after spending. With bank money investment can be many times that. It does not only pay for more production of the kind already being done. It pays for innovation, which further increases production.

The catch is that eventually too much bank money is created. Prices reach levels that cannot be sustained because they have to keep going higher to remain as high as they already are. When they stop going higher loans based on those levels cannot be paid back. Because loans cannot be paid back, banks suffer losses and are worth less. Consequently, they have to loan less. With less bank money available prices start to fall. They keep falling because the lower they get the less banks are worth, and the less they are worth the less banks can loan. The system collapses.

But the periods of prosperity more than offset the periods of recession or depression. Some of the increased production remains. Economies keep moving upwards despite the setbacks. Overall, production keeps increasing. It gets much larger than it would without bank money.

XXI.

Why Teachers Have Been Allowed To Teach Doctrines That Do Not Represent The Majority

Chapter 1

Why have teachers been allowed to indoctrinate students with their own beliefs when those beliefs have not been representative of the majority in their country?

Chapter 2

What teachers indoctrinate students with has been very much criticized because it was not representative. But these criticisms have not been acted on. The indoctrination by teachers has been allowed to continue.

Chapter 3

Teachers' power to decide what they indoctrinate their students with has developed only recently.

Minority rule was the prevailing form of government throughout the greater part of history. No public criticism of the minority rule was allowed.

Minority rule was necessarily accompanied by a certain morality. Morality and law both deal with controlling behavior. Children were educated by their families and communities and were taught to accept minority rule and its accompanying morality.

It was only within the ruling minorities that teachers as a special class came to exist. They were totally dependent on the minorities they served and so taught what those minorities wanted them to.

Minority rule had been replaced by democracy in many parts of the world. Democracy requires the expression of differences of opinion about what governments should do. This is essential for choices to be made by the public. To make this expression of differences of opinion possible there must be a degree of freedom of speech.

It is because of the necessity of freedom of speech that teachers came to be able to indoctrinate their students. No special restrictions have been placed upon them.

Chapter 4

Why did teachers have beliefs that were not representative of the majority in their country?

Chapter 5

Human beings developed a morality problem when they started living in collections of families.

Which they did in the agricultural age.

Originally, human beings lived in single families. They had no morality problem then. Their morality suited their circumstances. It took them through the steps of life.

The agricultural age caused human beings to live together in larger and larger groups. Which were made up of families like the families that had existed before. But for the first time they had to live with other families. The relations between the human beings making up these families were different than the relations of a single family.

Members of a single family have feelings for one another which make them willing to help one another. They do not have the same feelings for members of other families.

Before the agricultural age the feelings human beings had for other families were feelings of hostility. Because families competed for available resources and had to fight one another.

When the agricultural age made larger groups necessary, these feelings of hostility had to be repressed. There had to be a certain unity so they could oppose the other larger groups.

This forced a compromise. Families had to live together but they did not feel toward members of other families the way they did toward members of their own families and they did not treat members of other families the way they did members of their own families. The compromise was that families were responsible only for their own members. They could cooperate with other families under certain circumstances (in time of war, for instance), but otherwise they were on their own.

This would have been a simple enough arrangement if it had not been for a complicating factor. Human beings had developed imagination so they could think. But imagination could not be limited to thinking. It carried over to other parts of life.

With imagination human beings could put themselves in the place of others and have their own behavior determined to some degree by this.

That was what caused the morality problem. Human beings could not be completely indifferent to human being outside their own family. But at the same time they could not be completely responsible for those other human beings. Because of practicality. Adult morality had to somehow deal with this problem.

Childhood morality remained the same as it had always been. Because the behavior of children did not have to to change. The problem developed when male children became adults.

Male children because they were the ones who had to deal with relations outside the family. Female children did not. Their lives were confined to relations within the family.

Practicality and morality conflicted for men because there were not enough resources to go around. Competition was and is necessary for all species. But with human beings it became an even more difficult problem for the agricultural age. The agricultural age brought inequality. Human beings stopped limiting themselves to a subsistence level like other species. It became possible for them to get more than mere subsistence required. And there was no limit on how much more. This meant families could be in endless competition with one another. That part of life was dealt with by men. Childhood morality did not apply. It was not that men did not want to do well to others has they had been taught to do as children. It was that they wanted more to do well to their own families, including themselves. They had to use whatever methods worked. Which were often methods condemned by morality. For then there were two worlds. The world within the family. And the world outside the family. These worlds called for different and conflicting behavior.

Chapter 6

During the thousands of years of minority rule the compromise solution to the morality problem was a combination of charity and religion.

With minority rule childhood morality could not be applied to the adult world. The purpose of the minority was to exploit—the opposite of the purpose of the family.

Exploitation could be ameliorated with charity. Charity was voluntary. The amount could be better or less, depending on how much feeling there was for others. It never became so great that it interfered with the system.

Childhood morality was not renounced. The belief in it continued throughout life. The failure to practice it was excused by religion. Which put off the practice of childhood morality until after death. In another life.

Many found this to be an acceptable compromise. Those who did not were helpless. Minority rule could not be overthrown. And minority rule and childhood morality could not be reconciled.

Chapter 7

Democracy replaced minority rule because governments could no longer use force against their populations.

It was because minority governments had that capacity that they were able to rule for thousands of years.

When governments cannot use force against their populations, they have to get those populations to accept them voluntarily. This they do through democracy.

Chapter 8

Governments could no longer use force against their populations because of nationalism.

Nationalism developed spontaneously as communities within an area became less isolated. The people within that area came to have a feeling of national unity. They saw themselves as one people.

When isolated, communities have only a feeling of local unity. They identify with those in their own locality but not with those in other localities.

Governments promoted nationalism. It made possible national armies. Their populations saw themselves sharing interests they were willing to fight for. Once national armies became possible in one country, they became necessary for other countries. Which had to prevent themselves from being overwhelmed.

National armies had a consequence that was not foreseen. They could not be counted on to act against their own populations.

Throughout history areas had been conquered because

armies would act against the populations of other areas. Not only when wars were going on but after they ended. To the members of the victorious armies the populations of conquered areas had a different identity than they did.

Behavior toward them was different than behavior among themselves.

This distinction went back to the beginning of humanity. The members of the small groups human beings lived in had to fight their neighbors. There was not enough to go around. To fight their neighbors they had to be ready to inflict treatment on them they would not inflict on their own families.

Even then human beings had feelings of common humanity. But they had to be able to overcome those feelings. Which they could because of their feelings of separate identity.

With the development of nationalism those feelings of separate identity were replaced by feelings of common identity. Not altogether, but enough to make human beings within a country reluctant to act against one another as they used to. Their governments could no longer relay on them to do that.

Chapter 9

Once governments could no longer use force against their populations, basic differences of opinion developed.

Which was never allowed to happen with minority rule.

The first basic difference to develop was about how to divide up production. Those who were getting less began demanding more. The extreme form of this was communism, which called for equality.

The second basic difference to develop was about the responsibility of governments. Governments had not been held responsible for their populations. That would have been contrary to minority rule. Minorities ruled to serve their interests, not the interests of other members of their populations. When those other members came to share in the control of governments, as they did with democracy, they made governments responsible for whole populations. They replaced voluntary and incomplete charity with obligatory and complete charity.

The third basic difference to develop was about relations between men and women. Men had dominated women because they were stronger.

With democracy women prohibited the use of force in relations between men and women. This ended the advantage men had had and so ended their domination.

Curiously, this development was not foreseen. Men had gotten so used to their traditional relations with women that it never occurred to them that this could be changed.

Chapter 10

The new opinions appealed to childhood morality.

Childhood morality is family morality. It is what is suited to the functioning of the family.

The family divides up what is available so that all its members get enough. Since how much is enough varies with age and other circumstances, the family does not practice equality. It practices each according to his needs.

The family provides for all its members, not just some. Its responsibility is not limited. This is essential to the relationship between parents and children.

The family relies on authority. Each member cannot always do what he or she wants. Somehow the family must establish and maintain authority to deal with this problem. This makes children used to authority. But the authority they are used to is benign authority.

Chapter 11

Historically, human beings stopped practicing childhood morality—if they did—when they left childhood and entered the adult world.

This was a different process for them. Childhood is a very impressionable period. Its purpose is to teach children how to behave. It can do this only if they retain what they learn.

Until the rise of democracy only men—with few exceptions—entered the adult world. Women stayed within the family. So it was men who had to give up practicing childhood morality.

In earlier centuries those who found the process too difficult could turn to religion. Religion taught that childhood morality would be vindicated after death. Those who did adapt to the adult world used practicality to excuse their new behavior. They did what they did because they had to. They did not renounce childhood morality. They just stopped trying to practice it.

Once the new opinions that came with democracy developed, idealism replaced religion as the alternative for those who found the process of adapting too difficult. They wanted to change the adult world so it more closely resembled the childhood world. Unlike religion, idealism was usually temporary. The young men who espoused it tended to lose their dedication as they grew older and had more experience with the adult world. They came to accept that practicality would prevail—whether they liked it or not.

Chapter 12

Because teachers do not make their living dealing with the adult world, they tend to think childhood morality should be practiced throughout life.

Given that that is what they think, they indoctrinate their students with opinions based on the practice of childhood morality.

The majority of populations do have to deal with the adult world. They know childhood morality is not practiced in that world. They do not reject childhood morality outright, since that would go against their upbringing. But they accuse teachers of being impractical. Which is their way of saying childhood morality has to be compromised in adult life.

Chapter 13

Indoctrination by teachers was not controlled because of the cult of freedom of speech in democracies.

Democracies have to have (limited) freedom of speech so differences of opinion can be expressed. Otherwise, democracies cannot function.

All democracies have some limits of freedom of speech. But the pretense that limitations do not exist is usually maintained because popular issues have to be kept simple.

Teachers were not subject to any special restrictions because for a long time they posed no problem. They were conformist. Starting in the late 19th century, a few became non-conformist about some issues. But their numbers were small and they were not seen as a real threat. Then there was a change because of the Great Depression. Many teachers came to believe that whole economic system had to be reformed. After World War II they added the reformation of the social system because of the rise of women. They championed women's values.

These reforms started out as minority causes. Majorities supported traditional societies. But they were handicapped in their efforts to counteract the indoctrination by teachers because, traditionally, teachers had enjoyed the same freedom of speech as the general public. That they were in a special position with their students was not taken into account.

As generations of students entered the adult world, minorities favoring what teachers indoctrinated turned into majorities and majorities opposing this indoctrination turned into minorities. The teachers triumphed. Their values are the predominant public values in the modern developed world.

Chapter 14

The proponents of childhood morality believe in government intervention because they believe that in democracies governments can be made to do what their populations want and can be made to act in the interests of those populations.

They believe this because it is what they are taught. It is the theory of democracy. But it is believable only if not critical thinking is applied to it.

Populations in democratic countries have very limited control over their governments. It is more control than populations in non-democratic countries have, but it is not enough control so that governments can be made to do what their populations want and act in the interests of those populations.

Populations in democratic countries have very limited control over their governments because: The members of those governments are elected only at intervals. And the members of those governments can keep what they are doing from being known. And the members of those governments need large amounts of money to be elected and so much do what it takes to get these large amounts of money.

Representative government was developed because democratic government had become impossible.

Democratic government was possible when human beings lived in small groups. As they did for tens of thousands of years. The members of those small groups lived together and so could make decisions together. That was democracy.

When groups of human beings went from small to large, as they did in the agricultural age, members of those groups no longer all lived together and so could not make decisions together. They might come together at intervals, but during those intervals they had to delegate authority. They had to appoint others to act for them.

Representatives chosen at intervals can often do what they please because different situations occur during those intervals and they cannot be given instructions detailed enough to cover all of those situations. This means that those who choose them can only approve or disapprove of their general performance.

This was always a problem and became a much bigger problem in the modern era of big government.

The problem was aggravated because representatives in a democracy can keep secret most of what they are doing. The result is that the general public not only cannot deprive them of independent authority but lacks the information it would need to judge them.

At the beginning of modern democracy whoever was trying to get elected needed very little money for his campaign. There was practically nothing to spent it on. That did not means money did not enter into politics. It did. Politicians could be bribed. And were. But they did not need the money to be elected and re-elected. Now they do. Campaigning has become very expensive. Because politicians need money to campaign, money can control politicians. Those who give it will not give it for nothing. So the little control the general public used to be able to exercise over politicians has become less. Much less.

Chapter 15

While childhood morality is espoused, that has not changed human behavior.

The behavior of adults in the practical world is still determined by their self-interest, not by childhood morality.

What the espousal of childhood morality in the adult world has caused is more hypocrisy. The pretense of practicing childhood morality has to be maintained. That causes more hypocritical misrepresentation than traditional morality did. Less of reality can now be admitted.

XXII.

Why The Conventional Wisdom About Investing Money Is Wrong

Chapter 1

The conventional wisdom about investing is wrong.

Chapter 2

The conventional wisdom about investing is wrong because it is based on the assumption that stocks should be sold as well as bought.

Chapter 3

That stocks should be sold as well as bought seems too obvious to be a subject for discussion. But there is overwhelming evidence to prove that stocks should not be sold.

Chapter 4

Mutual funds provide the overwhelming evidence that stocks should not be sold.

Many propositions can be proved by logic alone. But that stocks should not be sold is not one of them.

Before mutual funds it was assumed that stocks should be sold as well as bought. It was taken to be common knowledge.

There was no reasoning to prove that this was false. There was nothing about stocks that would allow such a conclusion. On the contrary. Stocks are a subject about which knowledge can be acquired. Those with more knowledge are presumed experts. They should, presumably, be better able than non-experts to predict what stocks will do. So they should be better able to know when stocks should be sold.

But mutual funds have shown this not to be so.

Mutual funds attracted experts. Lots of money could be made by the management of mutual funds. There was plenty of competition for these positions. And there was plenty of knowledge to be acquired. Business schools sprang up more or less simultaneously with mutual funds. Degrees from them were highly valued.

Mutual funds had the opportunity to prove that experts could invest in stocks better than non-experts. The results would be conclusive. There came to be thousands of mutual funds. It would not be a case of a few examples whose results might be non-representative.

And there were results to compare them with. Information about stocks and their performance has become voluminous. So it was easy to compare the results of mutual funds with results that were obtained when stocks were just bought and not sold.

These comparisons were made frequently. There was great curiosity about stocks' performance because money could be made from guessing correctly how they would perform.

These comparisons showed that mutual funds did not do as well as collections of stocks that were not sold (Index funds.) The difference was not close. Results would vary from time to time but they tended to be in the 90-10 range in favor of index funds. So there was the overwhelming evidence that mutual funds underperformed.

Chapter 5

So why is it that holding stocks pays better than buying and selling stocks?

Chapter 6

Economies have grown. The assumption is that they will continue to grow.

The Great Depression caused doubt about economies growing. They shrank, they did not grow. It seemed that their growth was over.

Economics did not correctly anticipate that stocks would increase in value because it did not give sufficient importance to innovation. This was strange, since the Industrial Revolution took place because of innovation. But economics had a tradition of thinking that nearly all innovation that was going to take place already had taken place.

What is going to be innovated cannot be foreseen. If it could be, it would be produced. But while what is going to be innovated cannot be foreseen, innovation in general can be. This is because of the acquisition and sharing of knowledge in the modern world. Out of that knowledge have come new things and new ways of doing things. This has meant more production. It is assumed this increase in production will continue.

Chapter 7

The assumption that economies will grow makes plausible the belief that the value of stocks will increase and so they should be held rather than sold.

The return on stocks has been about 9 per cent a year since World War II. Of this 6 per cent has been in appreciation and 3 per cent in dividends.

That so many mutual funds have not been able to equal this return in the past indicates they will not be able to do that in the future.

Chapter 8

The return from stocks that are held can be increased by buying small amounts of stocks in proven companies.

Knowledge does not enable the experts to buy and sell stocks so that they show a higher return than the averages. But it does enable them to pick out the stocks that are most likely to do well in the long run. There is information which indicates this, while there is not information which indicates when stocks should be bought and sold.

The stocks most likely to do well in the long run are the stocks of large corporations which have been in business a long time. They have a known record of success.

It is not enough to just buy these stocks. Enough of them have to be bought in small enough amounts so that the poor showing of a few will have only a small effect on over-all results. This is contrary to conventional wisdom. Which is that investors should not buy more stocks than they can follow. That is part of the buy and sell thinking.

When an investor owns small amounts of many stocks the gains on those that do well will more than offset the losses on those that do poorly. Because only small amounts of many stocks are owned, the losses on a few will be small. But the gains on those that do well can be very large. Those bigger gains dwarf the little losses.

Chapter 9

So why is the conventional wisdom about investing the conventional wisdom? It is because brokerage firms and financial media make money from it.

Brokerage firms make money from the buying and selling of stocks. They do this through charging commissions.

The financial media make money through the buying and selling of stocks through the increased interest buying and selling cause in financial news. Investors who only buy stocks are not preoccupied with the latest developments. They do not have to pay as much attention to financial media.

Promoting the buying and selling of stocks is easy because the public intuitively believes that is how to make money in the stock market. The logic is simple. Agreement is general. It is not disputed.

Brokerage firms and financial media are well aware that mutual funds underperform the market averages. But they know the general public will ignore this if they do.

XXIII.

Why The Solution To The Alzheimer's Problem Is Suicide

Chapter 1

The solution to the Alzheimer's disease problem is suicide.

Chapter 2

Alzheimer's disease has become a crushing burden on modern economies.

Better living conditions are causing human beings to live much longer. The longer they live, the more of them contract Alzheimer's disease. The problem this creates has not been dealt with.

Chapter 3

Alzheimer's disease differs from most diseases in that it deprives the victim of personality.

It is as if Alzheimer's disease killed the individual without killing the individual's body. Those with Alzheimer's disease are no longer human beings in the usual sense of the word. They are bodies without personalities.

Chapter 4

The peculiar characteristics of Alzheimer's disease mean that those suffering from it have to take action about their fate while they still have the capacity to do so. If they wait too long, they will no longer exist as a personality. They will be incapable of action.

Chapter 5

The solution to the problem of Alzheimer's disease is suicide because the modern public finds it very hard, if not impossible, to inflict death.

The opposition to the death penalty illustrates this. The death penalty was accepted throughout history. There were and are practical arguments for it. But the responsibility for inflicting death, no matter what the circumstances, puts off the modern public. So much so that they will support convicted murderers for life rather than execute them.

Given democracy, there is no possibility that the victims of Alzheimer's disease will somehow be disposed of by governments. The certainty of this is assured because with the welfare state family members themselves do not have to pay to keep the victims alive.

Chapter 6

The condemnation of suicide has become anachronistic.

The condemnation of suicide existed because of the circumstances of an earlier period. This earlier period was one in which minorities ruled. Morality was what minorities wanted it to be. The morality condemned suicide because it would have deprived the ruling minorities of workers and soldiers. They lived from exploiting these workers and soldiers and, naturally, did not want them to destroy themselves. The possibility of this happening was very real because the workers and soldiers—and their families—lived miserable lives. Suicide would have been an escape for them. So it was discouraged.

The ruling minorities did not have to concern themselves with Alzheimer's disease. Life was too short for it to be a problem. The few cases that occurred were taken care of by the families involved, since families at that time were responsible for their own members.

With the advent of democracy morality came to be what majorities wanted. The old reasoning behind condemning suicide no longer applied. The common good was put first, not the good of a minority.

The common good calls for a solution to the problem of Alzheimer's disease because it has become a crushing burden for the community. And the burden will keep increasing unless something is done.

Chapter 7

Those coming down with Alzheimer's disease would serve the common good by committing suicide because this would prevent so much money from being wasted on them.

That is only half the benefit they would confer. The other half would be that this money would be available for other uses. Uses that would contribute much more to the common good.

Modern democracies have shied away from considering what other uses could be served by the money they spend on causes like keeping Alzheimer's disease victims alive. That is because the uses they do spend the money on are not chosen rationally. The choices are determined by a combination of popular sentiment and activism. No attempt is made to show they do more for the common good and other choices would.

Making money available from Alzheimer's disease could start serious debate of alternative uses. So much could be accomplished.

Chapter 8

Suicide has become painless.

This is an important breakthrough.

Suicide used to be painful. There is no way of knowing just how much of a deterrent effect this had. But it certainly had some. Not only was there the prospect of death. There was the prospect of suffering in order to die.

Today suicide can be achieved by taking pills that cause no pain.

This is an important breakthrough not just because of the elimination of pain. It also eliminates the need for an accomplice. Like a doctor. That need for an accomplice raised the issue of murder. Not only was there the difficulty of safeguarding an accomplice from being punished as a murderer. There was the danger that real murder could be committed and gotten away with because it could be made to look like suicide.

The painless, solitary suicide that has become available to all makes solving the Alzheimer's disease problem much more of a real possibility.

Chapter 9

Suicide as the solution to the Alzheimer's disease problem calls for a sense of responsibility on the part of the victims.

All creatures want to live. Life would not work if they did not. So anyone committing suicide has to overcome this natural attachment to life.

Most diseases cause pain. Often extreme pain. This makes their victims willing to consider suicide. And often to commit suicide. Death becomes preferable to the pain.

But Alzheimer's disease does not cause pain. So those

who suffer from it do not have the most effective motive for suicide. They continue to feel normal.

And Alzheimer's disease does not have obvious symptoms which warn when the critical stage is approaching. The stage when the victims are unable to make decisions. Once that stage is reached only death can release them.

That is why a sense of responsibility is called for. The victims must remind themselves that their continued physical existence would cost a large amount of money. Some or all of which would have to be paid by the community. They can vegetate on for years, since Alzheimer's disease itself does not cause death. They must remind themselves that this money could be spent for much better causes. Causes that without their cooperation otherwise would not get it. They could be benefactors. Benefactors on a very large scale.

And all victims must remind themselves that their physical survival would not be the survival of what they think of as themselves. Those selves—the selves they have known as themselves all their lives—cannot be saved.

XXIV.

Why Imagination Created The Future

Chapter 1

Imagination created the future.

The future does not exist for any species besides the human species. And it did not exist for the human species until that species acquired imagination.

Chapter 2

Imagination created the future because it enabled human beings to be conscious of more than the present and the past.

Most creatures are conscious of only the present. That does not mean the past does not exist for them. But it does through other means than consciousness. The past exists through their bodies. And this is so not only for their own bodies but for the bodies of their ancestors. Most of what they know they know through heredity.

Chapter 3

Imagination enabled human beings to be conscious of more than the present and the past because it enabled them to detach themselves from reality.

Most creatures are conscious of only reality. A few can be conscious of the past. There is evidence for this. But only human beings can be conscious of the future. Because of imagination.

Human beings developed imagination so they could make better choices. With imagination they detach themselves from reality. They can see the otherwise sense in imagination what they are not actually seeing and otherwise sensing at the time. By doing this they can manipulate the elements of their experience differently than those elements occurred.

This gives them more experience than they have actually had. And better choices depend upon more experience.

Throughout most of their existence human beings thought other creatures had a consciousness like theirs and could do what they did with their consciousness. There are many fables which bear this out. It is only recently that experiments have shown that these fables are based on a false understanding of other creatures. Their limited behavior shows that almost all of them have no form of consciousness.

That imagination created the future was accidental. Its purpose was to make better choices by manipulating experiences otherwise than they actually occurred. "What would happen if—" is how imagination works.

The future was a side effect of this new capacity. Human beings could ask "What would happen if—" about the future as well as about occurrences without relevance to time. And they did because it was of extraordinary usefulness to them.

Other creatures have to rely on the past repeating itself. Because their behavior is determined by what happened in the past. Not only to them but to their ancestors. (Through heredity.) Because the past does repeat itself to some degree it can seem that these creatures have anticipated the future and so chosen appropriate behavior. But that is not what happens. They are only successful to the extent that the past repeats itself.

Chapter 4

Imagination made the future causative for human beings.

Because human beings can imagine the future, they can plan their behavior to suit it. This is very different from relying on the past to repeat itself, as other creatures do. It gives human beings an adaptability no other species has.

Human beings cannot only imagine the future. They can imagine what they might do in the future and what results this would have. They can consider various possibilities and choose the one that seems most advantageous. This then causes them to act in a certain way.

Human beings take it for granted that the future is causative, because it has been for them for thousands of years. They do not appreciate the uniqueness of this situation. They do not appreciate how much it has contributed to their development.

XXV.

Why Peace Advocates Do Not Understand Why Peace Has Become Possible

Chapter 1

The peace advocates do not understand why peace has become possible.

Chapter 2

Peace has become possible because now more can be made from peace than from war.

It is as simple as that.

Chapter 3

The peace advocates believe that human beings can choose what they do and if they choose not to fight war there will be no war.

They think it is as simple as that.

It is not.

Chapter 4

Human beings can choose what they do.

Every human being knows this from personal experience.

There was some dispute about this during the long period of belief in an all-powerful supernatural creature. The reasoning was that human beings could not choose what they would do if this creature was truly all-powerful. Because then He would determine everything that happened. Including all human behavior. But this belief no longer prevails and now it is commonly accepted that, yes, human beings can choose what they do. Otherwise, intelligence would be useless.

Chapter 5

If human beings can choose what they do, why did they choose war?

Human beings have been in three different situations which provide three different explanations for their choices about war. The first was the situation that existed before they started living from agriculture. The second was the situation that existed while they were living from agriculture. The third is the situation today.

Chapter 6

Before agriculture, human beings lived subject to the same conditions as other creatures.

These were the conditions that made evolution work.

More young were born than could survive. The survivors had to fight for the means of subsistence. Fight within their own species and fight against other species. They had no choice about fighting. So whether they wanted to fight or not was irrelevant. They had to fight.

Chapter 7

Agriculture introduced inequality among human beings.

During the period before agriculture human beings lived in what amounted to single families. Except for the effects of differences in age, the members of families shared equally. None possessed more than others because they lived a subsistence existence. There was nothing to have more of.

The situation changed with agriculture. Human beings started living in collections of families. They did because agriculture made that possible and once it became possible it was necessary. They needed the numbers to survive against other collections of families.

The families in these collections lived separately from one another. They had to because their numbers forced them to spread out. This mean none could have more than another, since they were no longer sharing.

So agriculture brought inequality in possessions. But the other inequality it brought was even more important. This was inequality in power. More important because everything else was dependent on it.

Agriculture brought inequality in power because collections of families had to act together if their numbers were to be used effectively. Numbers by themselves could accomplish nothing. They had to be subject to authority. Then they could act together. And whoever had authority had power. Those organized numbers were power.

At the beginning collections of families were small and those exercising authority were few. With time the collections of families increase in size because the larger they were the more capable they were of defeating other collections of families. Getting larger was necessary for survival.

As groups of families got larger, the number of those exercising authority increased. It was impossible for one man or a few men to exercise authority effectively over larger numbers. Authority had to be delegated. One man gave orders to those immediately below him. They gave orders to those immediately under them. And so on.

Whoever exercised power could use it to get what he wanted. Including more possessions. Providing whoever already had those possessions did not have enough power to prevent this from happening.

Chapter 8

With agriculture human beings could live off one another.

Before agriculture human beings could not live off one another. They all had to work.

The changes that agriculture caused constituted a new situation. A minority could live off a majority. The minority did not have to work. The majority had to work.

Before agriculture when human beings had more food their numbers increased. This was evolution at work. It happened with all species.

In the new situation there was an alternative. Instead of an increase in numbers an increase in what workers produced. That was possible because fewer workers could produce more per worker. Human beings had been aware of this before agriculture. They had seen it over and over again in their daily experience with getting food. But it took agriculture to enable them to act on it.

That was because a minority was ruling. Thanks to concentrated power, they could reduce the number of workers. Then they could appropriate the extra production for themselves. Not only did they no longer have to work. They could have production put to other purposes than producing food.

Chapter 9

In this new situation wars had to be fought.

And were throughout the period when human beings lived from agriculture.

It was not because human beings were aggressive. It was because they had no choice. Wars wee necessary. Wars did not happen because human beings were aggressive. Human beings were aggressive because wars had to be fought.

Wars had to be fought because the groups human beings were living in had to get stronger to survive. The way to get stronger was to acquire more land that would produce more food. The way to acquire more land was to take it from others through war.

Chapter 10

The situation within countries was different from the situation between countries.

Within countries wars had to be minimized. Because they weakened countries and made them easier to defeat by other countries.

Despite this, wars were often fought within countries. This was because the members of the ruling minorities wanted to get more for themselves. And one way to do that was to take it from other members of those minorities within their own country. This could be easier than trying to take it from other countries.

Members of ruling minorities did not want more just because having more was a means of strengthening their country against other countries. They wanted more for the sake of more. For more possessions and more power. And not only because they wanted more for the sake of more but because the more they had the stronger they were within their own countries.

What enabled wars within countries to persist was that they happened in all countries. So that, as a general rule, no one country was weakened more than any other country. But while this was true generally it was not always true and countless countries were defeated, and often went out of existence, because they weakened themselves too much with internal wars.

Chapter 11

The necessity of war ended when it became possible to increase production without increasing land.

Providing the increase in production was more than it would have been from increasing land.

Which it came to be because of the Industrial Revolution.

This development is still not understood even though its results have been conspicuous in the 20th century.

Chapter 12

It had always been possible to increase production. And production had been increased throughout the period when human beings lived from agriculture. What changed was the rate of increase.

The rate of increase was what mattered. It had to be great enough so that because of it more could be made from peace than war.

Chapter 13

World War II was fought because of the old thinking. But after World War II the new thinking prevailed in advanced countries.

In advanced countries because it was there that the rate of production could be increased the most.

These countries realized that their strength and well-being were not going to increase by increasing their territories. Not as much as they would increase by increasing their production within the territories they already had.

War as a means of increasing national strength and well-being had become an anachronism in advanced countries.

That did not mean it had become an anachronism in general. Most countries were still not advanced to the extent they could always make more from peace than from war. And they still had beliefs left over from the previous period which made them ready to go to war for other reasons than increasing production.

The prospect was that the less advanced countries would become more advanced, as some of them were doing. And that they would leave behind the beliefs left over from the previous period.

Chapter 14

The peace advocates think that war has declined because of their argument that war is bad.

War was always bad. War always caused suffering and loss. War was not fought because it was popular. It was fought because it was necessary.

The peace advocates now have a good argument. Only they are not aware of it. They continue to think that war can be eliminated because it is bad. That has never worked. Behavior can change when conditions have changed. Conditions have changed because of the Industrial Revolution and its consequences. That is the argument for peace advocates to make. Peace is now possible. It is possible because it is more advantageous than war.

XXVI.

Why Speculation Creates Wealth Out Of Nothing

Chapter 1

Speculation creates wealth out of nothing.

Chapter 2

The wealth speculation creates has the same power to buy as the wealth created by production.

Chapter 3

Speculation causes prosperity. The more speculation, the better the times.

Chapter 4

The more speculators there are, the more money they can make. Whereas the more producers there are, the less money they can make.

Chapter 5

Speculation provides its own financing. It does not have to be subsidized.

Chapter 6

Speculation prolongs itself. The more it causes prices to go up, the more prices go up.

Chapter 7

Speculation is rational at the beginning. But it is irrational at the end.

Chapter 8

Speculation is the easiest way to make money.

Chapter 9

Speculation is the easiest way to get rich.

Chapter 10

While speculation causes crashes and slumps, it can have some positive effects.

Chapter 11

Speculation has to do with changes in prices. Changes in prices can take place without changes in what wealth consists of. So wealth can increase without any increase in what it consists of. It can increase out of nothing.

Chapter 12

Wealth is measured in money.

There is no practical way to measure wealth other than with money. Because wealth consists of what is diverse. Quantatively, comparisons can be made only with what is the same. That is why there is money.

Chapter 13

Speculation increases prosperity because it increases demand.

Speculation creates more wealth. More wealth means more demand. More demand means more prosperity. With more demand more is produced. When more is produced there is more prosperity.

Chapter 14

The more speculators there are, the more they can make.

In contrast with producers. The more producers there are of any given product, the less they can make. Because their competition with one another drives down prices. And so drives down profits.

The more speculators there are, the more they drive up prices. Because prices depend on demand. More speculators mean more demand, and more demand means rising prices. And rising profits.

Chapter 15

Speculation provides its own financing because the more prices go up and more can be borrowed against what is being speculated in.

Banks need security for their loans. The security for the loans that speculators get is whatever they are speculating in. How much that is worth depends upon how much speculation is taking place. The more speculation, the more it is worth. So as the speculation goes on the more can be borrowed to finance it.

Chapter 16

Speculation prolongs itself because the more it causes prices to go up the greater the expectation they will continue to go up. Which causes them to keep going up.

Chapter 17

Speculation is rational at the beginning because there have to be circumstances that cause a belief prices will go up.

If such circumstances did not exist, prices would not start to go up.

Once prices start to go up, there is less need for circumstances that seem to justify their rise. More and more speculation is based on the expectation that since prices have already gone up they will continue to go up. This can be rational enough for a while. But it becomes irrational when prices have gotten so high that the underlying circumstances provide no justification for them.

This does not mean that the speculation will stop. The irrational phase can continue for a long time. Much longer than the rational phase.

That is often overlooked after the crash. There is a tendency to look back and say that the speculation should have stopped when irrationality took over. But that is to misrepresent the situation. The greatest opportunities for making money come after irrationality has taken over, not before.

The difficulty in this situation is to know when to get out. That cannot be predicted. So many speculators keep speculating and get caught in the crash.

Chapter 18

Speculation is the easiest way to make money.

Speculators do not have to do any work. All they have to do is make a purchase. And then wait.

Speculators do not have to acquire any special knowledge. All they have to do is become aware that prices are going up somewhere in something. They can do this with general knowledge.

Then all they have to do is make that purchase.

Chapter 19

Speculation is the easiest way to become rich. With speculation a little money can make a lot of money in a short time.

Speculators can start with very little money. They can borrow to increase how much that little amount of money will buy. When they make their first sale they have more money. Then they can borrow again. This time they can borrow more than they did the first time. Because they have more money to put up. Then they can make a second sale. After which they will have more money. And so be able to borrow more money. They can go on like that indefinitely. Until they quit before the collapse or get ruined in the collapse.

Speculators can make a lot of money in a short time. Because prices rise fast. In contrast with making money in production. Production is slow because things have to be done that take time. With speculation nothing has to be done to make prices go up. It can happen from one sale to the next.

Speculations usually last only a few years at the most. But in that time many speculators become rich. And those who get out before the collapse stay rich.

Chapter 20

While speculation causes crashes and slumps, it can have some positive results.

Speculation increases production because it causes bank money to be created.

Bank money has the same effect on demand as government money. The more of it there is, the more demand there is. And the more demand there is, the more prosperity there is.

Government money is understood. Bank money is not understood.

Government money consists of pieces of paper that the government says should be accepted as having buying power.

Bank money consist of entries at banks which banks say have buying power. When banks make loans, they make new entries.

Governments can issue as much money as they wish. The only restriction on them—which they can ignore—is the consequences of issuing more of this money.

Banks can issue only a limited amount of their money. The limit is that how much they issue cannot exceed how much government money they have by a certain amount. This means they can issue much more of their money than they have in government money. Which means that the total amount of money out there can be much greater than the total amount of government money.

The total amount of government money is permanent. Once issued, it stays out there. If the pieces of paper this money consists of get too worn to be used, the government replaces them.

The total amount of bank money is not permanent. It goes up and down. It goes up when banks make more loans. It goes down when they make fewer loans. This is a very important difference between bank money and government money.

The bank money created by speculation increases the the total amount of money as the speculation goes on. This increases demand and production as the new money spread through the system.

When the crash comes much of the bank money disappears. The bank loans become worthless as prices fall. With the large decrease in bank money there is a large decrease in demand and production. A slump beings.

But the material wealth that was produced during prosperity does not disappear. This can offset to some extent the decreased production after the crash. As an examination of capitalist countries shows. So speculation can have some positive results.

XXVII.

Why There Is No Logically Defensible Morality Without God

Chapter 1

Who determines morality without God?

Chapter 2

One of the strangest phenomenon of modern times is the belief in morality.

Chapter 3

The belief in morality should have been challenged along with the belief in religion.

It has not been. Religion has been largely discredited. The belief in morality remains as strong as it was during the height of religion.

There is no evidence to indicate the slightest opposition to the belief in morality. It is simply not questioned.

Chapter 4

Without religion there is no argument for the belief in morality.

Chapter 5

The belief in morality comes from childhood training.

The training is so effective that very few human beings can overcome it.

Chapter 6

It was childhood training, not religion, that provided the belief in morality. What religion provided was the argument for the belief in morality.

Chapter 7

The argument religion provided for the belief in morality was God.

God determined morality. Those who believed in God had to believe in morality. They could argue about what behavior morality called for, but they could not argue about the existence of morality. If there was a God, there was morality. It had to be whatever He determined it to be.

Chapter 8

If religion had not been discredited, it would have had a hard time explaining the changes in morality.

How could God have been mistaken about what was right and wrong? Since He was infallible, He could not have been. But the changes in morality did take place and much of religion went along with them.

This would have been a serious problem for religion if it had not already been discredited. Because of that, the public did not pay much attention to religion's efforts to explain how morality could have changed.

Chapter 9

So if God does not determine morality, who does?

Chapter 10

Morality has become competitive. The various versions of morality are in competition for acceptance.

There is no established procedure for conducting this competition. Whatever measures are used that seem to work. No version gains unanimous acceptance. But sometimes a version gains enough acceptance so that it is the only one publicly allowed.

Chapter 11

Morality is not democratic.

Democracy depends upon allowing differences of opinion. Then the public can make a choice.

Morality allows differences of opinion only when forced to by circumstances. Morality believes that only one opinion is correct. Right is right. Wrong is wrong. It condemns other opinions. It suppresses them when it can. That is the nature of morality.

Chapter 12

Morality is enforced differently than it used to be.

When religions determined morality, they punished both behavior and opinion that did not conform. They went to any lengths to do this. It was considered an acceptable practice.

In the modern world morality suppresses the public expression of differing opinions. This is an adaptation to democracy, the form of government that prevails in advanced countries. Opinions that cannot be publicly expressed do not matter in a democracy.

This method of suppressing differing opinions spares

morality from the condemnation it would receive if it tried to use the old methods, which have been discredited. And, if anything, it is more effective.

With the new method morality can pretend to allow freedom of speech. It does not have to use old-fashioned censorship, since it controls access to the public. And it does not have to punish private speech, as authoritarian governments do.

Chapter 13

In the new situation activism determines morality.

There was to be a self-interest group behind a change in established morality. Besides self-interest, which unifies the group, it has to have money and organization, which gives it staying power. Changing established morality cannot be done in a short period.

The older generation resists changes in morality. Morality is taught, not thought out. Those who have been taught it and who have lived with it for much of their lives are not likely to give it up.

The younger generation is more amenable. Part of growing up is acquiring independence, and part of acquiring independence is rejecting authority. So what comes hard for the older generation comes easily for the younger generation.

At the beginning all changes in established morality are minority causes. And they are often minority causes when they succeed, since the process for making them the new established morality is not a democratic process. Once the new morality has become established, it can seem to gain acceptance rapidly. But this is at least partly an illusion. What happens is that opposing the new morality is publicly condemned, so that many of those who still oppose it do so only privately.

Traditional morality did not realize quickly enough that it was being seriously challenged. It had been accepted so long that many of its supporters took it for granted that it would continue unchanged. They did not oppose the activism of their opponents with sufficient activism of their own. By the time they realized their mistake the new morality was established.

Chapter 14

The public does not trouble itself about the nature of morality because it has no doubts about the existence of morality.

For the public morality exists. So asking whether it exists is pointless. The public has known about the existence of morality since early childhood. They have a certainty of its existence that comes from within.

If the existence of morality is a certainty, the only uncertainty is what behavior it calls for in various situations. That this behavior can change over time does not cause doubts in the general public about the existence of morality. They accept that it adapts, though adaptation is not reconcilable with the existence of the morality they believe in. It is something they know is so whether they can explain it or not.

XXVIII.

Why Americans Wrongfully Blame Themselves For Taking Their Country Away From The Indians

Chapter 1

Americans wrongfully blame themselves for taking their country away from the Indians.

Chapter 2

This is typical of the new morality in the United States.

Chapter 3

The new morality appeared in the United States after World War II. It is based on the assumption that what children are taught is good and bad should be accepted as good and bad by adults.

Chapter 4

Children are taught it is bad to take anything away from other children. That is why Americans blame themselves for taking away their country from the Indians.

Chapter 5

Americans did not blame themselves for taking land away from the Indians while this was happening.

The strong had always taken land away from the weak. That was how the world had been divided up. When the Europeans spread into new areas, they did not feel they needed to justify their behavior. What they were doing had always been done.

They did have a legitimate justification. Which they used because it made them feel good, not because they thought it was necessary. This legitimate justification was that they were bringing a better way of life with them.

Until Europe became capable of spreading to new areas, civilizations had been pretty much on the same level. But now Europe was unique. It could produce more than other civilizations because it had developed a more productive technology. That more productive technology provided the better life that the Europeans brought with them. They could argue—and did—that they were doing the natives a favor by making the more productive technology available to them. And that was how it turned out.

Chapter 6

Americans vilified the Indians while they were fighting them.

This is normal. All countries (and all groups) vilify their opponents. They do this so they can have the feelings appropriate to fighting and other forms of hostility. They never lack for justifications for the vilification because they themselves are the judges or whether their justifications are satisfactory.

Chapter 7

Why didn't the Americans make slaves out of the Indians?

The Spaniards enslaved the Indians in their part of the New World. This enslavement worked. It was large-scale and continued for centuries. It was the basis of the economy.

The Americans did not make slaves out of Indians in their part of the world because conditions were different. These conditions made the enslavement of the Indians impractical.

Indians could not be enslaved because it was too easy for them to flee. They were hunters. There were unsettled areas near them where they could flee to. If attempts were made to enslave them—and there were such attempts—they could go off to the unsettled areas. Where they would-be slave master did not dare to follow them. Since they were Indians territory and dangerous for white men.

The Indians in what became the Spanish part of the New World were farmers. They could not flee. There was nowhere to flee to where they—being farmers—could live. Since there was nowhere for these Indians to flee to, they had to endure slavery.

The American Indians would have been in a different situation if they had remained in the areas the Europeans (later the Americans) took over. Some of these areas in time got to be far away from the unsettled areas. It would have been much harder for the Indians to flee.

But the Indians did not stay. They were able to live elsewhere, so they went off. And the Europeans/Americans did not want them to stay. They wanted the land for themselves, and drove off the Indians who did not leave voluntarily. At the time of the American Revolution there were still pockets of Indians along the East Coast, but they were soon nearly eliminated. The new settlers and Indians did not live together.

This continued to be true as the United States expanded westward. And once the Indians were defeated, they were put on reservations. Which were separate communities.

Chapter 8

The Americans changed their attitude toward the Indians once the Indians were defeated.

This did not happen immediately. It could not happen while Americans were alive who remembered fighting with the Indians. Once that generation was dead, Indians were thought of as peaceful victims. The past was forgotten. It was then that Americans started blaming themselves for how they had treated the Indians.

Chapter 9

For Americans to blame themselves for taking the country away from the Indians, they have to believe the unbelievable.

The unbelievable being that, unless for them, the Indians would have been left in possession of the country.

The Indians were bound to be dispossessed once the country was discovered. Given their way of life, they could not possibly have defended themselves against the Europeans and their descendants.

This was not true of Mexico and Peru. The way of life there was not that different from the way of life in Europe at the time. Those Indians could have held out for much longer than they did. It was because of avoidable mistakes that they were conquered so quickly. They might have fought off the Spaniards long enough to borrow advances from western civilization and maintain their independence.

The way of life of the Indians in North American kept their numbers low. They had an initial numerical advantage of the Europeans but it did not last long. The Europeans kept arriving, so defeating and pushing back the Indians became easy for them.

What was true of Indians along the East Coast was true of them throughout the country. They never had a real chance of prevailing. Their defeat was only a matter of time. If the Americans (and their European ancestors) had not dispossessed them, somebody else would have.

Chapter 10

The mystery about the Indians in North America is why they were so backward. And therefore so vulnerable.

Indians had started crossing over to the American continent 30,000 years ago. So it cannot be argued that their backwardness was due to lack of time to develop.

Conditions in many parts of the American continent were favorable to the development of civilization. Including in the eastern part of what became the United States. The climate and the soil made agriculture possible. And agriculture was known. It even prevailed in some limited areas.

So why did agriculture not lead to civilization, as it did in other parts of the world? A possible answer is the profusion of game.

The profusion of game was one of the most remarked on characteristics of North America. Whereas the available evidence indicates there was no such profusion of game in the areas where civilization developed.

A profusion of game meant hunters could thrive and become relatively numerous. It would have been harder for farmers to defeat them.

In areas that did develop civilization farmers had been at a disadvantage in their struggle with hunters. Hunters move about in bands. They can outnumber farmer when farmers are working alone or in small numbers in their fields.

But if farmers can hold out for a time and increase their numbers, they can make the situation favorable for themselves. They can enlarge their groups by uniting separate families. Then they can create and maintain armies that can defeat bands of hunters and drive them off. The settled areas can prosper. They can get bigger and bigger.

The farmers in North American were apparently unable to reach the stage when the situation vis-a-vis hunters became favorable for them. Since the profusion of game made the hungers too numerous. Civilization could not develop. When the Europeans came, the Indians could not match them armed force for armed force. They were vulnerable. Separated into groups with small numbers, they were easy to defeat. They might come together for brief periods and offer some real resistance, but their way of life made it impossible for them to stay together. So their opponents had only to wait.

Chapter 11

After the Indians were defeated, programs were instituted to make them competitive. But these were abandoned.

Indians could not compete in the United States so long as they were living like Indians. Which was what they did on reservations, where they had been put by the government. In an effort to make them competitive, their children were sent to schools which were like the schools for white children. This was the only program which, logically, could solve the Indians problem.

But the program was resisted and finally abandoned. (There was a similar program in Australia, which was likewise abandoned.) The argument was made that the schools took the young Indians away from their families and cultures. Which was the idea.

Similar schools were established in Africa and Africans came out of these schools and provided the leadership for the new countries.

The young Indians went back to the reservations, where, like other members of their families, they have been supported by the government.

XXIX.

Why Human Beings Can No Longer Be Equal

Chapter 1

Human beings can no longer be equal.

Chapter 2

Human beings can no longer be equal because of hierarchy and inheritance.

Chapter 3

Inheritance can be done away with. But hierarchy cannot be.

Chapter 4

Human beings were equal until (approximately) the last 10,000 years.

Chapter 5

Human beings could never be completely equal.

To be completely equal they would have to be identical and they would have to be living in identical situations.

For evolution to work creatures have to be different and they have to be living in different situations. Then they and their species can change through the reproductive process.

Chapter 6

Until the last 10,000 years human beings were as equal as they could be.

They shared what they had. They shared power over one another.

In sharing what they had they did not share with absolute equality because their needs were different. Men and women needed more to eat than children. And so on. The equality they had was that they all had their needs met (when possible).

Besides food they all had more or less the same because they led a subsistence life. There was nothing for one to have more of than other had. Except for a few personal possessions, which did not compromise the basic equality.

As to power over one another. They lived together in small groups. Those groups often had to act together. Particularly in their food-getting and their relations with other small groups in their area.

Originally, strength determined who exercised power. But this did not list. The others in the group realized their numbers could offset individual strength. So the groups came to live together democratically.

While the strong were curbed, the weak were protected. Because the members of the group were dependent on one another for their survival. All the members of the group had to be kept alive so they could defend themselves against neighboring groups. Which meant have as many members (approximately) as those other groups. (Given the way human beings lived at the time, only small groups were possible. So their numbers remained approximately the same.)

Chapter 7

With agriculture human beings came to live together in larger groups. Those larger groups made hierarchy necessary.

Hierarchy exists because larger groups need to act together and no one can provide that unity of action by himself. He has to have subordinates. And the subordinates have to have subordinates. Power has to be delegated. There have to be levels of power.

This divisions of power gives the individual in the hierarchy personal power totally out of keeping with natural differences of power. Before agriculture individuals had superiorities in endowment that they could exploit. But the natural differences were not that great. Human beings were not the same. But the degrees of difference among them were limited. Agriculture changed this situation radically. It introduced differences in power among human beings unlike any other difference in the natural world.

With these differences in power human beings could never be equal again. Attempts were made to limit the differences, but they invariably failed because of the nature of the situation. Equality among human beings had ended.

Chapter 8

Hierarchy caused smaller numbers.

The members of hierarchies discovered how to exploit other human beings.

Exploitation—meaning living on the work of others—was now known before agriculture. Human beings lived on the subsistence level like other creatures. When more food was available, their numbers increased. When less food was available, their numbers decreased. This was how evolution worked.

Human beings knew that when more food was available, it took them less time to get what they wanted. But living a subsistence life as they did, they did not make much of this knowledge.

With agriculture human beings could have more food. At the beginning this would have caused larger numbers. But in time it occurred to members of the hierarchies that another use could be made of this abundance of food. If numbers were not allowed to increase, each worker would produce more than was needed to keep him alive. This extra production could then be put to other uses. Such as keeping the members of the hierarchies alive. Such as keeping other workers alive who could then produce something besides food.

Chapter 9

Why was it that numbers determined strength in the primitive age but not in the agricultural age.

If numbers alone had determined strength in the agricultural age, hierarchies could not have exploited their groups. Because that exploitation required numbers be kept down so productivity could be increased.

Numbers alone did not determine strength in the primitive age. Human beings had already made discoveries—like weapons—that added to strength in fighting. But while these discoveries provided an advantage, that advantage did not last long. Because all the human beings in an area quickly became aware of them and acquired them. So that numbers remained decisive.

It was not like that in the agricultural age. Surplus—the new element—went into determining the outcome of fighting. It paid for what supplemented numbers. So hierarchies could reduce their numbers to get that surplus and not become militarily weaker. In fact, they became militarily stronger. As history shows.

Chapter 10

Hierarchy caused inequality of possessions and inheritance.

The larger numbers of agriculture made separate communities necessary. Not all the members of groups could live in the same place. These separate communities could have been collectives like the single communities of the primitive age. But because of hierarchy that did not happen. The members of the hierarchies divided up possessions (primarily land) according to their position. Since they were the ones who exercised power, they could do this.

Once areas had been divided up among members of hierarchies, they introduced inheritance. Inheritance did not exist in the primitive age. There was nothing to inherit. Besides, perhaps, a few personal possessions. But once there was something to inherit, what became of it after death mattered very much to the living. This was an extension of the feelings that went with the human family. The continuation of the family had always mattered. The family could not have existed otherwise. When it became possible for the basis of that continuation to be made hereditary, human beings reacted uniformily. They instituted inheritance. They passed on the existing inequality to their children.

Chapter 11

Democracy did not restore equality.

The American and French revolutions had to have popular support to succeed. Revolutionary wars are different from national wars in that there is government to provide an army. With revolutionary wars the armies have to be made up of volunteers, and without popular support there will be no volunteers.

To get popular support the leaders of both the American and French revolutions promised equality.

The American colonies did not have nearly as much inequality as France. Many of the Americans owned their own property and provided their own livelihood. Since property was readily available in a new country. France was an old country. Property was owned by a ruling minority, which took a large share of the proceeds for itself and gave those doing the work very little. All the inhabitants of America, except the slaves, were treated the same under the law. England had done away with different treatment under the law for different classes, and that part of its system had been adopted in the colonies. Whereas in France there was still different treatment for different classes. Government in France was run by the ruling minority. The remainder of the population controlled no part of it. In America much of local government was representative. But the heads of the colonies were appointed by a foreign king. He headed a representative government, and so could not be completely arbitrary, but that government represented his population, and only a small part of that population, so the Americans could do little to restrain him. Except protest. (Which the French were not allowed to do before the revolution.)

So the promise of equality meant more in the French Revolution than in the American Revolution. But in neither one did it mean anything like real equality. Hierarchy and inheritance remained.

There is a tendency to think that in the United States equality meant at least that every man (unless a slave) had the right to vote. But this is not true. States had property qualifications for voting. Not all white men could vote. Probably less than half could.

Property owners were afraid that the property-less would take their property away from them if they could vote. This was a very present fear wherever democracy was introduced. It proved to be a false fear. Because most members of the post-revolutionary populations could themselves acquire property. (Though usually not much.) So the vote was given to more and more of these populations, until everybody really did have the right to vote.

But what democracy showed was that voting by itself does not provide much control over governments. It happens only at intervals. It can be ignored for the most part. Money and pressure groups have much more to do with democratic governments than voting.

The French and American revolutions really did not mean to bring equality. That they would was an illusion used to get popular support.

Once the revolutions were won, equality continued to be proclaimed. And the publics continued to like that illusion of popularity. That it was only a illusion did not deprive it of all its appeal.

Chapter 12

Democracy did not end inheritance.

Democracy would have had to end inheritance for even a pretense of equality. Inheritance and equality cannot co-exist.

Inheritance gives some members of a population advantages that the other members of the population do not have. There is no limit on how great these advantages can be. Those who enjoy them can go through life without doing anything useful. They can buy whatever there is to buy. They can live at the highest level possible. They can get favorable treatment wherever they go. And they can pass on all these advantages to their children. Or to anybody else they choose. And this can go on indefinitely, generation after generation.

While equality is impossible with inheritance, there is not popular support in democracies for abolishing inheritance. It seems to be a natural right.

Once inheritances reach a certain point, they tend to get bigger and bigger. This point is reached when the heirs can live as comfortably, or as luxuriously, as they want from the income provided by their inheritance. Then any greater income from the inheritance can be invested. Most families can invest only a small part of their income, so their total investment remains small, and the part of their total income they get from that investment remains small. But families that can live on what they consider a satisfactory level from their inheritance are in a different position. They can get richer and richer, since the return on investments keep multiplying. And they can become very rich indeed as one generation follows another.

This great wealth not only provides them with a special kind of life. In addition, it enables them to promote their interests, since democratic politics depend so much on money. Needless to say, one of their interests is keeping the taxation of inheritance low, to the point of eliminating it. And they have been quite successful at doing that. Consequently, inherited fortunes have been growing throughout the world. With the inevitable negative effect on equality.

Chapter 13

Even if inheritance were abolished, hierarchy by itself would continue to make equality impossible.

Hierarchy necessarily causes an unequal division of power. Which carries over into the division of wealth.

Communist countries maintained that they had brought

about real equality in wealth by minimizing differences in pay and by ending private property.

They did, in fact, come closer to economic equality than any other form of society in the modern world. But they were unable to prevent hierarchy and the power that goes with it from being exploited.

Power is valuable. The favorable use of power will be paid for one way or another. So those in a government hierarchy can get something for the favorable use of power.

Hierarchies can try to prevent this from happening. At the beginning of communist rule, when idealism was at its height, hierarchies had some success at this. But as time went on idealism waned. Then the system itself aggravated the situation. Because it was those in the hierarchies themselves who had to prevent the abuse of power, and if they did they were acting against their own interests and those of their colleagues. Consequently, the abuses tended to get greater and greater as time went on.

XXX.

Why The Potentiality Of The Book Has Not Been Fully Exploited

Chapter 1

The only place where thinking can thrive is the book.

Chapter 2

The book is the only place thinking can thrive because it makes up for the deficiencies of the other forms of presentation.

Chapter 3

The greatest problem for thinking is the imperfect state of memory.

Memory is incomplete and unreliable. Human beings cannot remember everything. And what they remember they often remember inaccurately.

Thinking consists of a succession of thoughts. For an examination of thinking to take place, that succession of thoughts has to be remembered. This is often impossible if memory is the only form of preservation of those thoughts.

Chapter 4

The book makes up for the imperfect nature of memory.

Like memory, the book preserves that otherwise would be lost. But this form of preservation is complete and reliable.

Which means it makes available the succession of thoughts that thinking consists of. So that thinking can be properly examined.

Chapter 5

The human species has relied mulch more on physical memory than on mental memory.

Almost all species have to rely entirely on physical memory, since they have no mental memory. The human species as in the same position earlier in its existence. But once it developed consciousness and could think, it had an alternative.

With thinking the human species could discover new things and new ways of doing things. But in earlier times this did not happen very often. What did happen was that when a discovery was made, because human beings lived together in small groups, this discovery could be shared. The actions necessary to put this discovery into use could be taught. Others in the group were shown what to do. They repeated what they were shown. Which they could do because they had physical memory. Then, in time, they taught their children. And so the discovery became part of the general knowledge of the group, transmitted from generation to generation. Because of physical memory, not because of mental memory.

Chapter 6

With writing the human species could rely more on mental memory, because writing can make up for memory's failure to be complete and reliable.

But writing came later in human development. And its use was confined to a small minority. So its effects were very limited. It was not until printing that writing became available on a larger scale. And not until the 19th century that it was generally usable as an alternative to speech.

Chapter 7

When printing became generally available, the potentiality of the book was not fully exploited.

Books continued to use presentations of thinking like those of public speeches and private conversations. Human beings were used to such presentations and did not allow sufficiently for their deficiencies.

Public speeches are not meant to present thinking. They rely on feeling.

Feeling preceded thinking in human development. It told human beings what to do. It put them in physical states suited to whatever that was. Thinking was an improvement on feeling. It provided more successful reactions. But feeling did not go away. Thinking had to overcome feeling when the two were in conflict. And often it failed to do that.

With public speeches audiences do not have to remember sequences of thought. (Which, because of the limitations of memory, they could not do.) They have only to maintain whatever feeling the speakers are relying on. It is comparatively easy for speaker to get them to do this. Conflicts between feeling and thinking are not noticed at the time. Feeling triumphs.

Feeling dominates private speech even more than it does public speech. The private speakers say what they are for or against. They may express that as arguments, but this is only a pretense. Logically, feeling cannot be argued about. (Though it is all the time.)

The book offered an escape from this situation. Because it can present a succession of thoughts. (Which can be remembered because they can be reviewed at any time.) And because books can lessen feeling. Feeling runs higher in personal confrontations. It is not absent when arguments are made in print, but it tends to be less intense.

The potentiality of the book can be fully exploited when

feeling is not involved. As it is not in many subjects. That is why science has made such progress.

Feeling is involved when subjects have to do with human behavior. If that feeling is allowed to intrude in books that deal with these subjects, the reasoning will be advocates' reasoning, not real reasoning.

Advocates' reasoning is reasoning meant to achieve an object. It is selected for that purpose.

Real reasoning is reasoning meant to determine the truth and so increase understanding.

Unfortunately, advocates' reasoning has not been excluded from books on subjects that have to do with human behavior. The potentiality of the book has not fully exploited. So far, a great opportunity has been missed.